Make Money With Your Service Department

An Effective in-depth Management Tool For The Service Director/Manager

JEAN-CLAUDE DEMONT

Outskirts Press, Inc.
Denver, Co'

GW00801676

Acknowledgements

This book could never have been completed without the support and assistance of my wife, Hitiura, as well as the support of my wonderful daughter Michelle. Hitiura has helped in countless and immeasurable ways, and Michelle left her dad out of several school projects to prepare this book. Families play an integral role in dreams, aspirations, and accomplishments. My mother has always instilled me the importance of education, hard work, and discipline. My father, who was an automobile technician, introduced me to the automobile technology at a very early age, and made me one of the best automobile technicians. For that, I could never thank them enough.

My first employer had a profound influence on my life. Every day, to and from high school, from the bus window I used to look at an automobile dealership, where the owner was also a race car driver, and I told myself, "When I graduate, I will work at his dealership." After graduation, I met with the owner, and worked for him for several years. As a race car driver, he taught me the winning attitude needed to succeed.

I had the privilege in my early managerial career to work

many years for the French automobile manufacturer RENAULT, which was a pioneer in the matter of automobile dealership service and parts departments management. There, I learned the fundamentals that allowed me to develop my own methods, which I have applied over the last 30 years. I am particularly thankful to Gérard Dosmond, Gustave Verdier, Jean-Pierre Arzalier, as well as Jean-Pierre Nicolas.

Finally, I am obliged to the many people I have met in the course of my working life, for the conversations, questions, and shared insights that contributed to shape this book.

Introduction

At a time where several specialized organizations reported that automobile dealers' profits declined to a five-year low in 2005, and almost a third of them lost money, I believe there are better ways. One of them is definitely by considering the service department as a "profit center" and by managing it efficiently. The purpose of this book is precisely to present the options you have as a service director/manager to manage efficiently your service department, and bring your shares to maximize the overall profit of your dealership

If you have been in the business for a while, you probably have noticed that each automobile manufacturer calls the same thing something different, and here is where the difficulty starts. In most other industries, indicators and benchmarks are set from the government or associations, business schools, etc. The procedure to manage a service department is not unanimously defined, and almost every automobile manufacturer has its own way of doing things, its own way of requesting information from its dealers, and its own terms to define the same functions, or at least to get the same results. Keep in mind that even though terms and procedures are different, the principles are the same. The only differences reside in the definitions and the benchmarks.

We encourage you to contact your vehicle manufacturer, local dealer association, or local Automobile Association to get these benchmarks and compare them with your figures to pinpoint strengths and weaknesses in your service department.

In this book, I start at the beginning and allow the methods I have used to manage several profitable service departments unfold to the end. I use the most common and logical terms, and you will find their definitions in the glossary at the end of the book.

Also, we are going to crunch numbers for a while, but hang in there; in most cases, you will be able to download spreadsheets or programs to help you when you go back to your shop.

People expect the service director/manager to be a magician:

- The customer wants the best repair quality in the shortest possible time, and the cheapest possible way.
- The dealership principal wants the best possible customer retention rate, no customer complaints, and a maximum profit.
- The vehicle manufacturer wants basically what the customer wants and, on top of it, limited warranty expenses.
- The parts manager wants a minimum inventory and maximum profit.

- The technician wants to make the most money he/she possibly can, with the minimum effort.

As a service director/manager, you are confronted on a daily basis with these different needs from different people, but remember you are the magician, and you will find in this book what it takes to pull out of your hat the "magic" people expect from you!

Contents

Chapter 1

EVERYTHING IS ABOUT HOURS

Every business sells something to make a profit. What does a service department sell? ***HOURS!***

Hours are sold to customers through invoices, to manufacturers through warranty claims, to your company's other departments through internal billing. Labor is charged by the hour, technicians are paid by the hour, warranty claims are billed by the hour. In a service department, everything is about hours. In this chapter we will discuss the different categories of hours, their definitions, and their relationships.

Before we begin, let us clarify a common misconception: we tend to associate 1.25 hours to an hour and 25 minutes. Yet, 1.25 hours does not mean 1 hour and 25 minutes. In order to make the hour more "manageable," the decimal system is used (100th equal 1 hour). We proceed by dividing 100th by 60 minutes. The resulting number is an approximation of 1.66. Although the answer is incredibly close to 1.66, it does not reach 1.66.

Consider the following: 50th in the decimal system equals ½ hour, or 30 minutes. If we divide 50th by 1.66 = 30.12, the number that results is very close to 30 minutes, yet not exactly 30. This is the reason for the common ambiguity that arises when we end up with different results.

Time Conversion	
100th	Minute
5	3
10	6
15	9
20	12
25	15
30	18
35	21
40	24
45	27
50	30
55	33
60	36
65	39
70	42
75	45
80	48
85	51
90	54
95	57
100 © JcDemont	60

TABLE 1-1 Hundredth/Minute conversion table.

To conclude the matter, the 1.25 hours mentioned earlier should be interpreted as the number of hours, here 1, and the 25th converted to 15 minutes (as $25 \div 1.6666 = 15$ minutes). To sum up, 1.25 hours thus equals 1 hour and 15 minutes.

1.1 FLAT RATE HOURS (FRH)

The automobile manufacturers establish fixed times for most conceivable repairs. This includes everything from a bulb replacement to installing a new engine. These times are used for billing as well as paying purposes for the operations performed by technicians; they are referred to as Flat Rate Hours. Manufacturers reimburse warranty works based on these times. Dealerships mark up these times by 1.2, 1.5, or more to bill a customer (in some countries in which efficiency is very low, we found coefficients as high as 2.5). Automotive technicians are generally paid according to the amount of work they do; this system is known as Flat-Rate Compensation.

First, let us discuss the relationship with the warranty. The manufacturer repair time for a given operation is 3.50 hours. The dealership will charge the manufacturer, and will be paid for 3.50 hours. The technician who performed the job will also be paid a maximum of 3.50 hours regardless of the time spent performing the task.

Now, the customer paid bill. The manufacturer repair time for a given operation is 3.50 hours. The dealership will charge the customer $3.50 \times 1.2 = 4.20$ hours. The technician who accomplished the job will also be paid a maximum of 4.20 hours regardless of the time spent on the task.

1.2 AVAILABLE HOURS

The *Available Hours (also called Available Time)*. It can be defined as the time your shop is open for business, multiplied by the number of technicians.

In order to accommodate several objectives, it is possible to have daily, weekly, monthly, or even annual available hours.

Consider the following example: your shop is open 8 hours a day, 5 days a week, and it is closed 10 days per year for holidays. Also, bear in mind that you have 10 technicians.

Your shop's available hours will look like this:

- **Daily**: 8(daily hours) X 10(tech.) = *80 Daily Available Hours.*
- **Weekly**: 80(daily avail. hours) X 5(days worked per week) = *400 Weekly Available Hours.*
- **Monthly**: 400(weekly avail. hours) X 4.33(average weeks per month) = *1,732 Monthly Available Hours.*
- **Annual**: 1,732(monthly avail. hours) X 12(months)= 20,784 – 800((80 daily avail. hours) X 10(holidays per year)) = *19,984 Annual Available Hours.*

1.3 FIXED NON-PRODUCTIVE HOURS

Do your technicians spend 8 hours on site every day of the year that your shop is open for business? NO, they are awarded vacation days, training days, and other planned off-time. These hours are frequently called FIXED NON-

PRODUCTIVE HOURS.

1.4 ATTENDANCE HOURS

When you deduct the Fixed Non-Productive Hours from the Available Hours, you obtain the ATTENDANCE HOURS, which represent the time your technicians are present on site.

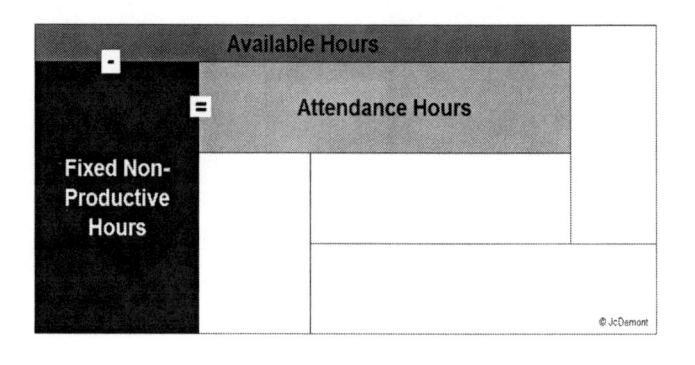

FIGURE 1-1 Available hours – Fixed non-productive hours = Attendance hours.

1.5 VARIABLE NON-PRODUCTIVE HOURS

Then, unfortunately, your technicians may be present on site, but do not spend every hour working on vehicles. The time wasted between jobs, either waiting for parts, or other non-productive tasks, is often referred to as VARIABLE NON-PRODUCTIVE HOURS.

1.6 PRODUCTIVE HOURS

Now, when you deduct those Variable Non-Productive Hours from the Attendance Hours, you will obtain the PRODUCTIVE HOURS. You are probably thinking: "Finally! Something productive!" I got you.

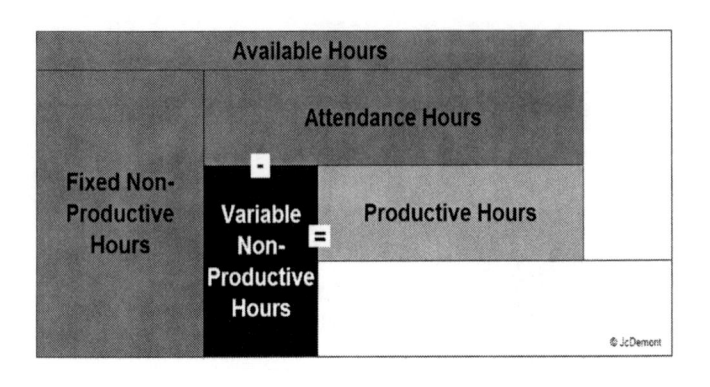

FIGURE 1-2 Attendance hours – Variable non-productive hours = Productive hours.

If your technicians are paid on a fixed salary, you probably scratch your head and come to realize all the hours you need to sell to compensate for these non-productive hours. If your technicians are paid by flat rate, you probably feel relieved!

Before we discuss the last category, let us look at a real-life example:

Our example shop:
Open 8 hours/day, 5 days/week (8 X 5) = 40 weekly hours.
Close 5 days/year for holidays (8 X 5) = 40 hours.
Staff: 10 technicians.
Training: 5 days/year per tech. (8 X 5) X 10 = 400 training hours.

Paid Vacation: 5 days/year per tech. (8 X 5) X 10 = 400 vacation hours.
Average waiting time at the parts counter: 10 minutes.
Average waiting time between jobs: 5 minutes.
Average jobs performed by technician per day: 6.
Average shop efficiency: 133%.
Effective Labor Rate: $103.

First, we must evaluate the annual available hours:
40 hrs/week X 52 weeks = 2,080 hrs.
2,080 hrs – 40 hrs (holidays) = 2,040 hrs.
2,040 hrs X 10 techs. = **20,400 hrs.**

Next, we calculate the Fixed Non-Productive hours:
400 training hrs + 400 hrs of vacation = **800 hours.**
Our shop attendance hours are 20,400 – 800 = 19,600 hours.

Now, let's deduct the Variable Non-Productive Hours:
5 days/week X 52 weeks = 260 days.
260 - 5 days (holiday) = 255 days.
255 - 10 (5 days vacation/tech. + 5 days training/tech.) = 245 days.
Each technician works 245 days per year.
Each technician does 6 jobs per day, so 6 X (5 minutes lost between jobs) = 30 minutes/day/tech.

If we consider that each technician is very well organized, that there is no additional work, and that he/she makes only one trip to the parts department per job, the time spent at the counter is: 6 X 10 minutes = 60 minutes/day/tech.
Each tech. loses (60 min. + 30 min.) = 90 min. or 1.5 hours/day.
Our shop Variable Non-Productive Hours are (1.5 hrs X 10

tech) X 245 days = **3,675 hours**. Ouch!

You now have a pretty good idea of the cost of a poorly managed Service Department. In our example, only 5 minutes are lost between jobs and 10 minutes wasted to get parts at the parts counter. You need almost 2 additional technicians to compensate this wasted time!
Our shop's productive hours are 19,600 – 3,675 = 15,925.

1.7 PRODUCTIVITY

You always hear about productivity. So what is our shop's productivity? Easy, it's the *Productive Hours* divided by the *Available Hours*, then multiplied by 100. Thus (15,925 / 20,400) = 0.7806 X 100 = **78.06%.**
Our shop's productivity is 78.06%.

1.8 TECHNICIAN UTILIZATION

Technician utilization is another important but less-known factor, and it gives you a pretty good picture of your internal organization. It is obtained by dividing the Productive Hours (the time your technicians work productively) by the Attendance Hours (the time they should be working) X 100: (15925 / 19600) = 0.8125 X 100 = **81.25%.**
Our shop's technician utilization is 81.25%.

1.9 SOLD HOURS

All right! Now, let's talk about the hours we like as Service Directors/Managers: The Sold Hours. They include the hours billed by your department to customers, to the manufacturer, and to your company's other departments. They are the ones that bring money to your department and your profit if you manage your department efficiently.

Did we just refer to efficiency? So, how do you tell if your shop is efficient or not?

The **EFFICIENCY** that everyone involved in management is talking about is the product (%) of the *Sold Hours* divided by the *Productive Hours*. Unfortunately, it is the last step of the process!

Figure 1-3 shows clearly the difference between the productive and the sold hours; this gap is your efficiency. Of course, the greater the efficiency, the greater your profit will be.

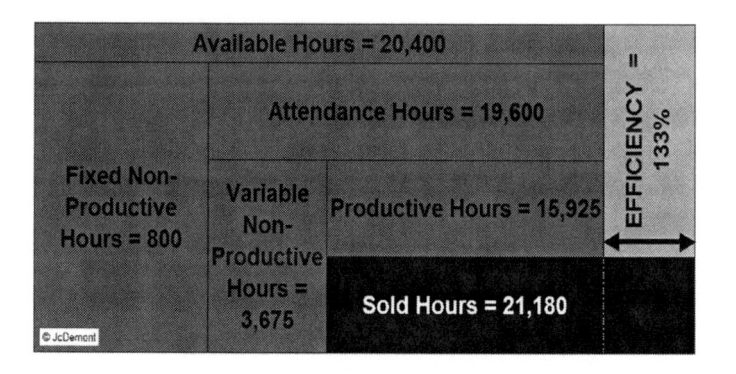

FIGURE 1-3 Sold hours – Productive hours = Efficiency.

Let's see what our Labor Sales is:

15,925 (productive hours) X 133% (efficiency) = 21,180 hours sold.

$103 (ELR) X 21,180 = $2,181,540.

Our shop's total labor sale is $2,181,540.

Let me explain the expression of the previous paragraph that says, "unfortunately, it is the last step of the process. " By this I mean that after this step, nothing else can be done to improve your department's profit. Good managers know that. They not only focus on the efficiency, but also on the entirety of the points previously discussed.

2.0 PROFICIENCY:

Proficiency is another quick and powerful indicator to gauge the health of the entire shop or a technician's output. It combines Productivity and Efficiency, and it is obtained by dividing the Sold Hours by the Available Hours.

Let us see how our example shop did:

21,180 (sold hours) / 20,400 (available hours) = 1.04 X 100 = 104%.

Not so well! You are looking for a 120% proficiency on a well-managed shop.

Before we close this chapter, you must understand the importance of all the points covered previously.

Consider the following two examples using the same data

as our example above. The first example demonstrates a change in *Available Hours* (by including working hours also completed on Saturdays). This setup increases our shop's Labor Sales by almost $500,000 annually. See Table 1-2.

	Our Example Shop			By adding Saturdays	
Data		Math	Data	Math	
Daily open Hours	8		8		
Weekly working Days	(5)		(6)		
Close for Holidays (day)	5		5		
Number of Technicians	10		10		
Available Hours		20400		24560	
Training (Day/Year/Tech.)	5	40	5	40	
Paid Vacation (Day/Year/Tech.)	5	40	5	40	
Fixed Non-productive Hours		800		800	
Attendance Hours		19600		23760	
Avg. Waiting time at Parts counter (min)	10	16.67	10	16.67	
Avg. Waiting time between Jobs (min)	5	8.33	5	8.33	
Avg. Jobs/Day/Tech.	6		6		
Technician # of annual working Days		245		297	
Variable Non-Productive Hours		3675		4455	
Shop Productive Hours		15925		19305	
Avg Shop efficiency (%)	133%		133%		
Total Hours Sold		21180		25676	
Effective Labor Rate	$103.00		$103.00		
Total Labor Sales		$2,181,586		$2,644,616	21.22%

© JcDemont

TABLE 1-2 Available hours increased by working on Saturdays.

The second example displays a change in *Variable Non-Productive Hours* (here the waiting time at the parts counter has been reduced from 10 to 5 minutes). This setup increases our shop's Labor Sales by almost $200,000 annually. See Table 1-3.

Our Example Shop			With Parts Waiting Time Reduced to 5 minutes		
Data		Math	Data	Math	
Daily open Hours	8		8		
Weekly working Days	5		5		
Close for Holidays (day)	5		5		
Number of Technicians	10		10		
Available Hours		20400		20400	
Training (Day/Year/Tech.)	5	40	5	40	
Paid Vacation (Day/Year/Tech.)	5	40	5	40	
Fixed Non-productive Hours		800		800	
Attendance Hours		19600		19600	
Avg. Waiting time at Parts counter (min)	10	16.67	5	8.33	
Avg. Waiting time between Jobs (min)	5	8.33	5	8.33	
Avg. Jobs/Day/Tech.	6		6		
Technician # of annual working Days		245		245	
Variable Non-Productive Hours		3675		2450	
Shop Productive Hours		15925		17150	
Avg Shop efficiency (%)	133%		133%		
Total Hours Sold		21180		22810	
Effective Labor Rate	$103.00		$103.00		
© JcDemont Total Labor Sales		$2,181,586		$2,349,392	7.69%

TABLE 1-3 Variable non-productive hours decreased by reducing the waiting time at the parts counter.

In conclusion, efficiency should not be the only source of concern. You must analyze your shop numbers frequently, and look for ways to increase Available and/or Attendance Hours, and ways to reduce Fixed and/or Variable Non-Productive Hours. Managing the hours is your first step in managing your service department efficiently.

Chapter 2

SERVICE MARKET POTENTIAL

The automotive repair business is huge. According to the US Department of Commerce, in 2002 Americans spent $120 billion on motor vehicle repair services. They spent another $49 billion on tires, parts, accessories, and lubricants. Clearly, new-car dealers have the opportunity to capture more of this business if they can compete effectively.

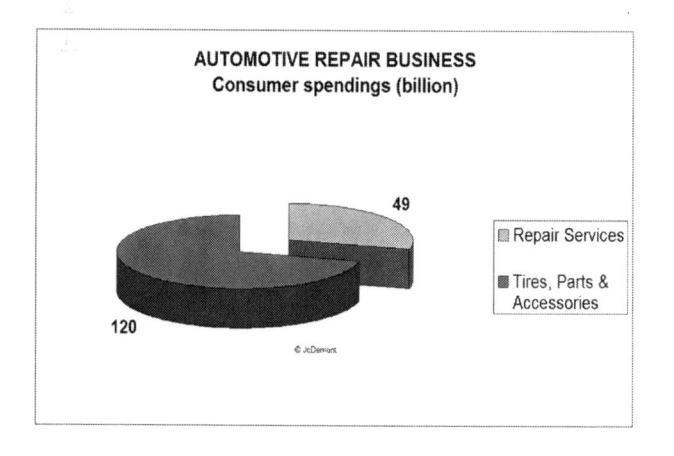

AUTOMOTIVE REPAIR BUSINESS
Consumer spendings (billion)

49

120

Repair Services

Tires, Parts & Accessories

© JcDemont

The revenue from business generated by Service Departments and Parts Departments frequently represents an extremely profitable area for vehicle manufacturers and dealerships. In order to maximize the profits, the service director/manager must know the sales potential of his department and establish a solid base needed to elaborate a successful evaluation of the shop capacities (work force, area, equipment, parking, etc.).

Thus, the *Service Market Potential Analysis* evaluates the labor and parts needed to maintain a given owners base (also called "Car Park").

You must agree that the knowledge and awareness of the number of customers' cars you must maintain, the number of hours required to maintain those cars, and the number of technicians needed to perform the required tasks, form the foundation of the service business. You would be surprised to know that many dealership service directors/managers do not evaluate their sales potential, and are convinced that they excel in their services to their customers when they only fulfill 35% of their potential!

When questioned, some Service Directors/Managers have a pretty good idea of how to perform this analysis. They use the number of new cars sold by their dealership during the last five years, then multiply this number by the average time required per vehicle to properly maintain it (this information is available from the manufacturer or the Dealer Association), and voilà!
Here is an example:

- Car Park (cars sold by dealership for the last 5 years): 12,000.

- Average labor (hours) needed to maintain a vehicle for 5 years: 55 hours.
- 55 hours X 12,000 = 660,000 hours.
- The Annual Labor Potential is 660,000/5 years = **132,000 hours**.

Then, to obtain the Labor Sales Potential, you multiply your Effective Labor Rate (ELR) by the Annual Labor Potential hours.
To obtain the Parts Sales Potential (by Service department), you would multiply the Labor Sales by the Parts/Labor ratio (average 0.80).
By adding Labor Sales and Parts Sales, you would obtain your Service Market Potential.

Your Labor Sales potential is ($100(ELR) X 132,000 hours) = $13,200,000.
Your Parts Sales potential is ($13,200,000 X 0.80) = $10,560,000.
Your Service Market potential is ($13,200,000 + $10,560,000) = $23,760,000.

This is by far the most popular procedure used today to evaluate the Service Market Potential, and there is a reason for this:

The general public tends to shun the new-car dealer franchises for everything except warranty work and complicated repairs. They perceive these dealers as very expensive places to have their cars worked on.

Also, according to the latest (as I write) JD Power and Associates "Service Usage and Retention Study," fewer than half of non-luxury vehicle owners remain loyal to new-car dealers for service after the fourth year of vehicle ownership.

Dealers retain only 66 percent of annual service visits in the first year of ownership, falling to 55 percent by the third year. By the time most customers come off warranty in the fourth year, the dealer's share of service visits falls to 47 percent.

We believe that by using this procedure, the service director/manager loses the rest (all cars older than 5 years old) to his competitors, and that is why we recommend that you use a different approach to this analysis.

The U.S. Department of Transportation reports that the average life span of a vehicle is just over 13 years, with a final mileage of 145,000 miles. Half of all registered vehicles are at least 8 years old, a third of them 10 years old or older. The average new-car buyer trades in the car at 55,000 miles, approximately every 4 years.

If your objective is to focus on your 5-year owners base, you are missing 8 years of Labor Sales. Also, keep in mind that as cars get older, they require more maintenance and repairs. So these 8 years should be the most profitable years for your service and parts departments.

When conducting such analysis, I use the 10-year Car Park (10-year owners base), which I divide in 3 segments. The first segment includes 4 years of sales; the second segment includes 3 years of sales, and finally, the third segment similarly also includes 3 years of sales. The number of years adds up to 10:

- Segment 1: Cars up to 4 year old.
- Segment 2: Cars between 5 and 7 year old.
- Segment 3: Cars between 8 and 10 year old.

An impressive number of cars are seriously damaged during accidents and natural disasters, and are scrapped each year. Let us keep this factor in mind. It is an important factor in some countries, where we found a 10% Annual Scrap Rate!

Here is the list of what we need to conduct such an analysis.

You need from the sales department:

- Previous year's total new car sales.
- Year - 2 total new car sales.
- Year - 3 total new car sales.
- Year - 4 total new car sales.
- Year - 5 total new car sales.
- Year - 6 total new car sales.
- Year - 7 total new car sales.
- Year - 8 total new car sales.
- Year - 9 total new car sales.
- Year - 10 total new car sales.

Then, you will need to get the *average annual scrap rate* in your state, country, or area from DOT, dealer association, insurance groups, etc.

Let us look at another example:

2.1 CAR PARK (Owner base)

- Previous year total new car sales = 2800 vehicles.
- Year - 2 total new car sales = 2600 vehicles.
- Year - 3 total new car sales = 2500 vehicles.
- Year - 4 total new car sales = 2300 vehicles.
- Year - 5 total new car sales = 1800 vehicles.
- Year - 6 total new car sales = 1600 vehicles.
- Year - 7 total new car sales = 1500 vehicles.
- Year - 8 total new car sales = 1300 vehicles.
- Year - 9 total new car sales = 1000 vehicles.
- Year - 10 total new car sales = 800 vehicles.

TOTAL= **18,200 vehicles**

Segments:

- Segment 1: (2800+2600+2500+2300) = 10,200. (56% of total).
- Segment 2: (1800+1600+1500) .... = 4,900. (27% of total).
- Segment 3: (1300+1000+800) ....= 3,100. (17% of total).
- Annual Scrap Rate: 4% (18,200 X 4%) = **728**.

Car Park (owners base): 18,200 – 728 = 17,472.

2.2 LABOR POTENTIAL (hours)

Annual Average Labor (Hour) needed to maintain a car: 11 hours.

Older cars require more repairs:

- Segment 2 requires around 10% more than Segment 1 = 11 X 10% = 1.1 hour.
- Segment 3 requires around 15% more than Segment 1 = 11 X 15% = 1.65 hour.

- Segment 1: (17,472 X 56%) = 9,784 X 11 hrs = 107,624 hrs.
- Segment 2: (17,472 X 27%) = 4,717 X 12.1 hrs = 57,076 hrs.
- Segment 3: (17,472 X 17%) = 2,970 X 12.65 hrs = 37,570 hrs.

Total = **202,270 hours.**

2.3 SERVICE MARKET POTENTIAL

Labor: ($100(ELR) X 202,270 hours) = $20,227,000.
Parts: ($20,227,000 X 0.80) = $16,181,600.

Your Service Market Potential is ($20,227,000 + $16,181,600) = $36,408,600.

Yes, gentlemen, this is your market potential! Unfortunately, you do not retain 100% of your customer base, but as service director/manager, you must focus on customer retention to grab shares of segments 2 and 3.

Offering your customers lower Labor Rate as well as discount prices on parts for segments 2 and 3 can help you accomplish this.

As you probably know, it is possible to offer segment 2 and 3 customers a lower labor rate, and still maintain your actual Effective Labor Rate. Go to Chapter 11, *Effective and Variable Labor Rates* for proper procedure.

In conclusion, remember that as service director/manager, you must focus on customer satisfaction to increase their loyalty to your dealership. You are responsible for bringing some of these customers back to your shop!

Chapter 3

FACILITY POTENTIAL AND UTILIZATION

In the chapter *Service Market Potential*, we discussed the market potential based on your Car Park (owners base). Thus we are aware of the number of hours needed to maintain these vehicles. Your next step as a service director/manager is to know if your facility allows you to service these vehicles. The purpose of the Facility Potential and Utilization is just that. Is your service facility large enough to service the amount of incoming work? Is your service facility underused? Does it cost you too much money?

To evaluate the potential, and percentage of utilization of your facility, we are going to need some numbers from the Service Market Potential Analysis. Remember that in our example, we used a 10-year Car Park (10-year owners base). Also, we used a 4% Annual Scrap Rate, and a $100 Effective Labor Rate. The end results resemble this:

- The total Car Park was 17,472 vehicles.
- The annual Labor (Hours) potential to maintain this Car Park was 202,270 hours.
- The Annual Labor Sales were $20,227,000.

We know that we have to service a Car Park of 17,472 vehicles, which represents an annual labor of 202,270 hours. Our next step is to evaluate the potential of our facility. In order to do so, we need few data from our facility. The first set of data will include the number of bays available to service these vehicles (do not include car wash or other bays not used to service cars). Then, we need the Available Hours of your business. If you do not remember what Available Hours are, refer to Chapter 1, *Everything is About Hours*.

Business Annual Available Hours:

- Monday to Friday (5 days/week).
- Daily from 8a.m. to 6p.m. (10 hours).
- Closed 5 days/year for holidays.
- 5(days/week) X 52(weeks/year) = 260 days/year – 5(holiday) = **255 days/year.**
- 10(hrs/day) X 255(days/year) = 2,550 hours/year.

3.1 FACILITY POTENTIAL

Your shop is open for business 2,550 hours per year. Remember, from Chapter 1, to obtain the available hours, we multiply the business hours by the number of technicians. Thus for the Facility Potential, we will multiply the business hours by the number of available bays.

Let's look at the following example:

Your shop has 40 working bays: 40 X 2,550 = **102,000 hours**.
Your shop has 80 working bays: 80 X 2,550 = **204,000 hours**.
Your shop has 100 working bays: 100 X 2,550 = **255,000 hours**.

3.2 FACILITY UTILIZATION

To calculate the extent to which you use your facility, divide the Labor Potential (Hours) by the Facility Potential, then multiply the result by 100.

Your shop has 40 working bays: (202,270 / 102,000) X 100 = 198%.
Your shop has 80 working bays: (202,270 / 204,000) X 100 = 99%.
Your shop has 100 working bays: (202,270 / 255,000) X 100 = 79%.

Your Facility Utilization should be around 100% for optimum use, but not under 70%.

Let's go a little further. On the above example, with a Facility Utilization of 198%, the shop with 40 bays cannot service the volume of vehicles. What can the service director/manager do to service the customers? You are probably thinking: "He can move to a larger building." But, is there any available building around? Is the dealership principal ready to lease or purchase another building? Can the company afford that move?

Unfortunately, it is not that simple. The service director/manager must evaluate all possibilities before asking the dealer principal to approve of such a big modification.

Let's look at some options:

The service director/manager's first initiative was to open the shop on weekends:

- 2 (additional days/week) X 52 weeks = 104 days/year.
- 10 (hrs/day) X 104 = 1040 additional hours.
- 2550 + 1040 = 3590 hrs X 40 (bays) = 143,600 hours.
- 202,270 / 143,600 = **140%.**

The above option, with a 140% Facility Utilization, did not solve the problem. His second initiative is to create two shifts:

- The first shift will begin at 6:00a.m. and end at 3:00p.m. (9.00 hours).
- The second shift will start at 3:00p.m. and stop at midnight (9.00 hours).
- The shop will now be open during an additional 8.00 hours daily (18 – 10).
- 8.00(additional hrs.) X 255(days/year) = 2040 additional hours.
- 2550 + 2040 = 4590 hrs X 40 (bays) = 183,600 hours.
- 202,270 / 183,600 = **110%.**

The two options detailed above did not seem to solve the problem either. So, his third initiative is to include two shifts and to also open his shop on Saturdays:

- 1 (additional day/week) X 52 weeks = 52 days/year.
- 18 (hrs/day) X 52 = 936 additional hours.
- 936 hrs X 40 (bays) = 37,440 hours.
- 183,600 (hrs from 2nd shift) + 37,440 (hrs from Saturdays) = 221,040 hours.
- 202,270 / 221,040 = **91%.**

Congratulations! The service director/manager has finally found a solution to serve the dealership's customers. This example was used to illustrate the process involved in such instances of problem solving.

The Market Potential considers that you maintain 100% of your clientele, which is far from realistic. For instance, if we take an average of 60% customer retention, using our above example, to which we would add an additional day of work per week (Saturday), our 40-bay shop will look like this:

- Labor Potential: (202,270 hrs X 60%) = **121,362 hours**.
- Facility Potential: (102,000 hrs / 5(initially worked days/week) X 6(new weekly schedule) = **122,400 hours**.
- Facility Utilization: 121,362 / 122,400 = **99%.**

Now, what can you do when the Facility Utilization is below 70%?

- If your new-car sales are growing rapidly, and you have just moved to a larger facility, keep in mind that this is just a temporary situation. Try to find additional work to bridge the gap.
- Make sure you did not assign too many bays per technician.

You are probably wondering why I mentioned a $100 Effective Labor Rate, as well as $20,227,000 in Annual Labor Sales at the beginning of this chapter, and why we have not used those numbers yet.

Here is the answer: some manufacturers use a different approach to calculate the Facility Utilization, and use the dollar amount instead of the hours as we just did. The results are identical, but we will detail this method nonetheless.

Let's compare:
Our 40-bay shop example (done with hours)

- A Labor Potential of 202,270 hours.
- A Facility Potential of 102,000 hours.
- The Facility Utilization was (202,270 / 102,000) X 100 = **198%.**

Our 40-bay shop example (done with dollar amount)

- A Labor Sales of $20,227,000.
- A Facility Potential of (102,000 hrs X $100 (ELR)) = $10,200,000.
- The Facility Utilization is ($20,227,000 / $10,200,000) X 100 = **198%.**

In conclusion, if your Facility Utilization is below 70% or above 100%, you should analyze your numbers. Don't be afraid to put several solutions on paper! You will eventually find the right one!

Chapter 4

KNOW YOUR COMPETITION

Several factors have brought strong competition for your Service Department.

- The first one was the enormous size of the automotive repair business. According to the US Department of Commerce, in 2002 Americans spent $120 billion on motor vehicle repair services.
- Then, customers were not satisfied with the way dealerships' service departments handled customer service. Dealerships were too rigid, and not convenient; the relationship with the customer was not friendly, customers felt that they were only a number; often, the service was not fast enough, repair quality did not meet their expectations; and finally, repairs were too costly.

I used the past tense in the previous paragraph because dealerships improve their service everyday. Manufacturers offer several programs like longer contractual warranty periods, extended warranty, and all-included scheduled maintenance for new vehicles, as well as pre-owned ones, to prolong customer loyalty. Also, Customer Satisfaction Surveys are presented directly by the manufacturer or private companies hired by the manufacturers and they monitor their dealers' network with the Customer Satisfaction Index (CSI). A good CSI generally means additional incentives from the manufacturer for the dealership.

At the dealership level, efforts are made to improve a customer's experience with the service department. Service Advisors are required to build a good relationship with their customers, and make sure customers are satisfied. For a Service Advisor, a good CSI is an important criterion in keeping his/her job. Also, more and more dealerships offer extended working hours, going from extended evening hours, to a service department open 24/7. According to the May 2004 edition of the NADA Industry Analysis, 61.5% of dealerships offer extended working hours. See Figure 4-1.

SERVICE DEPARTMENT HOURS OF OPERATION

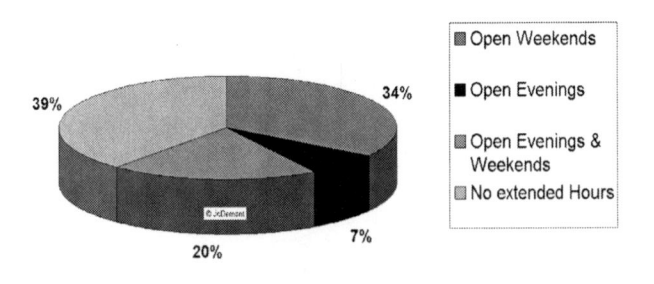

FIGURE 4-1 Service department hours of operation.

The gap between dealerships and their competitors is decreasing in matters of customer service and convenience, but price and speed of repairs are still at the advantage of service providers.

It is a shame that dealerships do not focus more on these two important factors, which can be seriously improved by offering a quick service (no appointment), and a variable Labor Rate, with lower rates for competitive and maintenance work. Go to Chapter 11 for more information on this subject.

As we previously mentioned, the first main reason why there is so much competition in the automotive repair business is the size of the market. Unfortunately, this is not going to decrease. Thus, as a service director/manager you won't be able to change anything about it. Secondly is the customer service (convenience, relationship, speed of repairs, price), and here you can do a lot to reduce the gap between your service department and the competition. You have a tremendous advantage in comparison with your competitors; you have the technical support of the manufacturer, a manufacturer maintenance program, the latest equipment, the best-trained technicians, and probably the nicest facility. But keep in mind that if you do not meet or exceed your customers' expectations, they will go to your competitors. So, understanding the competition facing your company is the first step toward offering your customers what they like about your competitors.

With a good understanding of the competition facing your company, you'll be able to use their strengths and weaknesses to your advantage.

Now, how are you going to map out the competitive landscape?

- First, make a list of all your current competitors, and research any that might enter the market within one year.
- Create a file for each competitor, and store the information gathered in it.
- Research competitors' strategies and objectives from their annual reports. Are their businesses growing, steady, or declining?
- Collect and study competitors' means of advertisement (flyers, newspaper, yellow pages, magazines, auto shows, expositions, etc.).
- Establish a list of the five services you would like to offer at your shop. Usually, they are brakes, exhausts, oil services, A/C, and tires (including alignment).
- Ask a person whom you know you can confide in to contact your competitors from a personal phone, fax, or by visiting them. Find out the prices they charge for these five services, what warranty they offer, what kind of mobility they offer while the customer's car is at the shop, the necessity of the appointments, and record the information on the *Individual Competitive Analysis* sheet shown in Table 4-1.

INDIVIDUAL COMPETITIVE ANALYSIS

Competitor Name: Date:

1. Price (List below can be changed)	This Competitor	Your Dealership	Difference		Your Advantage
Front Brake Pads replacement	$82.00	$86.99	$4.99	6.09%	NO
Rear Muffler replacement	$289.00	$320.00	$31.00	10.73%	NO
Oil & filter change	$29.99	$26.00	-$3.99	-13.30%	YES
A/C compressor Replacement	$345.00	$385.00	$40.00	11.59%	NO
4 wheels alignment	$69.99	$99.99	$30.00	42.86%	NO
TOTAL	$815.98	$917.98	$102.00	12.50%	NO
2. Warranty (Day)	90	365	275		YES
3. Convenience	Enter 1 for Yes, & 0 for NO				
Location	1	0	-1		NO
Access	0	1	1		YES
Near Public Transportation	1	1	0		NO
Loaner Vehicles	0	0	0		NO
Shuttle	1	1	0		NO
Customer Lounge	1	1	0		NO
Lounge comfort	0	1	1		YES
Fast Service	1	0	-1		NO
No appointment	1	0	-1		NO
TOTAL	6	5	-1		NO
Are your Prices competitive with this Competitor?	NO		OVERALL SCORE		
Is your Warranty better than the one from this Competitor?	YES		Your Dealership	4	
Are you more convenient to Customers than this Competitor?	NO		Your Competitor	13	

	This Competitor	Your Dealership
STRENGTHS (from Customer's viewpoint)	Very well located, courteous employees, quick service	Manufacturer backed up, factory trained Techs, original parts, latest equipment, lounge with comfort & internet, loaner fleet, courteous employees
WEAKNESSES (from Customer's viewpoint)	Oil service, brakes & alignment only	By appointment only, No walk ins, no quick service, difficult access because shop overload, and higher Prices
STRATEGIES & OBJECTIVES	Plan to offer exhaust repairs within 2 years. Increasing business.	Company plans to build another building which will improve access, and offer a quick service

Your comments: © JcDenient

TABLE 4-1 Sample of individual competitive analysis sheet.

- Next, put yourself in your customer's shoes, and drive around each of these competitors. Ask yourself if the location is good or not. Is the building nice and well maintained? Is it easily accessible? Is there a bus or a metro station located nearby? Record your findings on the *Individual Competitive Analysis* sheet.

- Then, visit them, or if you are well known, send a trusty and competent person to visit them, and look around for cleanliness and lounge appearance. Does the lounge offer wireless Internet access to its customers? Ask that person to observe the employees' interaction with the customers and to investigate customers' opinions about the quality of work, the staff, and prices. Also, ask them what they like and dislike about these companies. Record your findings on the *Individual Competitive Analysis* sheet.

Now, you should be able to evaluate strengths and weaknesses for each competitor. Then, by comparing them to yours, you will prepare a plan to challenge their strengths, and capitalize on their weaknesses.

Complete the *Individual Competitive Analysis* sheet for each competitor, report each sheet to the *Competitive Analysis* sheet, and store the individual sheets in their respective files.

You now have a review of all your competitors on one single sheet that looks like the one shown on Table 4-2.

COMPETITIVE ANALYSIS

Dealership: Date:

COMPETITOR NAME	Front Brake Pads replacement	Rear Muffler replacement	Oil & filter change	A/C compressor Replacement	4 wheel alignment	WARRANTY (day)	Location	Access	New Public Transportation	Loaner Vehicles	Shuttle	Customer Lounge comfort	Fast Service	No appointment	STRENGTHS (from Customer's viewpoint)	WEAKNESSES (from Customer's viewpoint)	STRATEGIES & OBJECTIVES
			PRICE							CONVENIENCE							
Competitor 1	$80.00	$199.00	$19.99			365	Y	Y	Y	N	N	N	N	Y	Y	Very well located, courteous employees, quick service	Not a full service facility, no transportation	Do not plan to make any change, will continue with existing clientele
Competitor 2			$16.99			90	Y	Y	Y	N	N	Y	N	Y	Y	Very well located, courteous employees, quick service	Oil service, minor maintenance only	Plan to stay as an oil service facility. Stable Business.
Competitor 3	$65.00	$200.00	$20.00		$59.99	365	Y	Y	Y	N	N	Y	N	Y	Y	Good location, service, warranty & prices. Fast service	Dirty & noisy lounge, not a full service facility	Declining business, looking for potential buyers.
Competitor 4	$75.00	$220.00	$24.99	$429.00	$99.00	365	N	N	Y	N	N	Y	Y	Y	Y	Good quality/price ratio, excellent warranty, offer transportation	Difficult Access, customers need to make a U turn on a very busy road	Plan to move to a better facility in a near future.
Competitor 5			$24.00			90	Y	Y	Y	N	N	Y	N	Y	Y	Very well located, courteous employees, quick service	Oil service, minor maintenance only	Plan to stay as an oil service facility. Stable Business
Competitor 6			$15.96			90	Y	Y	Y	N	N	Y	N	Y	Y	Very well located, courteous	Oil service, minor maintenance only	Plan to stay as an oil service facility. Decreasing
Competitor 7	$80.00	$245.00	$24.99	$399.00	$69.99	180	Y	Y	Y	N	N	Y	Y	Y	Y	Well located, good work quality, quick service	Employees with poor attitude, lack of management warranty	Do not plan to make any change, will continue with existing setup
Competitor 8	$79.99	$219.99	$22.99	$410.00	$59.99	365	N	N	N	Y	Y	Y	Y	Y	Y	Good quality/price ratio, excellent warranty, offer transportation	Badly located	Company is looking for a new location, but cannot afford to buy, will rent
Competitor 9	$60.00	$239.00	$20.00		$39.99	30	Y	Y	N	N	N	Y	N	Y	Y	Good location. Quick and cheap service	No transportation, use cheap quality parts, limited warranty	Will continue to advertise heavily to maintain Business shares
Competitor 10	$78.00		$24.99		$59.99	90	Y	Y	Y	N	N	Y	N	Y	Y	Very well located, courteous employees, quick service	Oil service, brakes & alignment only	Plan to offer exhaust repairs within 2 years. Increasing business.
Average Price	$74.00	$220.50	$21.49	$412.67	$64.83	203	80%	80%	80%	10%	10%	90%	30%	100%	100%			
Your Dealership	$99.99	$299.00	$29.99	$545.99	$99.99	365	Y	N	Y	Y	Y	Y	Y	N	N	Manufacturer backed up, factory trained Techs, original parts, latest equipment, lounge with comfort & internet, loaner fleet, courteous employees	By appointment only. No walk ins, no quick service, difficult access because shop overload, and higher Prices	Company plans to build another building which will improve access and offer a quick service
Difference	17.6%	35.6%	39.6%	32.1%	54.2%	79.8%					← 3.2w ioid							
Count	7	6	10	3	6	10	8	8	8	1	1	9	3	10	10			

TABLE 4-2 Sample of competitive analysis sheet.

Basically, you will find everything found in the individual sheet. At the bottom of the page, the line *Average Price* displays your competitors' average price for each selected category. In the blink of an eye, you will be able to compare them with your prices found on the next line.

Also, on the right of the average price line, the percentage for each "convenience point" is indicated. Here again, in a split second, you will know what your competitors offer. In our example, in Table 4-2, only 10% of our competitors offer *Shuttle service*, and 100% of them offer *Fast service* and *No appointment*.

The purpose of the next line, *Difference*, is to inform you of the gap between your prices and the average prices, and to help you adjust them accordingly.

The last line, *Count,* also shows where you have more competition. In our example, you have only 3 competitors in the A/C category, and 10 in oil service.

In conclusion, review your competition regularly, and do not delegate the job of keeping up with competitors. As a service director/manager, you are in the best position to appreciate and act upon information about your competition.

Chapter 5

MANAGING EMPLOYEES

The first step in managing employees is to ensure you hire the right person for the right position. The best way to succeed in this step is to prepare a job description for each position in your service department. Nobody knows your department like you do, so you must be able to write effective job descriptions.

If you plan to be ISO certified, each position must have a job description; it is one of the requirements.

5.1 THE JOB DESCRIPTION

A job description describes the major areas of an employee's job or position. A good job description includes the purpose of the job (the principal tasks involved for the position), the job requirements (knowledge and qualifications needed to succeed in the position), the relationship with other jobs in the company (can include the position this one must report to), the job responsibilities (a list of detailed responsibilities), and the ongoing responsibilities (communication, relationship, deadlines, etc.).

In addition, the job description can also indicates:

- The position of the immediate supervisor.
- The position that substitutes the latter.
- The signature, power, and authorization rights (limited purchase orders, limited correspondence, etc.).

Preparing a job description is a tedious task; yet, in the end, it is all worth it. A job description prevents you from hiring the wrong person for the position, and also clarifies any existing ambiguity concerning the specific duties and responsibilities. A job description must evolve according to the needs and requirements of your department.

To save you time, you can download job descriptions for almost all positions found in your service department at www.FirstAutomobileConsultants.com. As you know, needs and requirements differ from one another, and these job descriptions need to be adapted to the particular needs of your service department.

5.2 EMPLOYEE or INDEPENDENT CONTRACTOR

The second step is to evaluate if you want an employee or an independent contractor for the specified position. Whether a person is an independent contractor or an employee generally depends on the amount of control exercised by the employer over the work being done. Dictating how a job is to be done or limiting the actions of the worker may establish an employer-employee relationship.

An employee:
- *Performs duties dictated or controlled by others*
- *Is given training for work to be done*

An independent contractor:
- *Operates under a business name*
- *Invoices for work done*
- *Has own tools and sets own hours*

Independent contractors should not be considered as substitutes for regular employees. Government agencies generally find that people in the work force are illegally employed for tax purposes. The cost of being wrong, remitting unpaid payroll taxes, interest and penalties can be very high. You can find additional information at your local Small Business Administration office. They are a great resource.

5.3 INTERVIEW PROCESS

Interviewing candidates for a position within your company is one of the final steps in the hiring process. Before you get to this step, you want to ensure that you have already completed a job description for the position, that you have evaluated the salary for the position *(based on similar positions inside your company, as well as in the marketplace)*, that you have reviewed all applications and resumes, and have selected the few ones who match the job description for an interview. Then prepare yourself for the interview:

- First, make sure you know all the requirements and responsibilities for the position by reviewing the job description *(bring the job description to the interview)*.
- Second, the right candidate will have done some research on your company prior to the interview, and will ask you several questions regarding the position as well as the company, and the manufacturer you represent. Make sure you know all major facts regarding them.
- Then, prepare a list of questions based on the job description, the candidate's resume, and the culture of your company.
- Set a business-like atmosphere. During the interview, collect pertinent information, and observe the candidate's behavior patterns.
- Since you want to know about the candidate, my suggestion is that you use the 80/20 rule, which implies that you speak 20% of the time and let the candidate express himself the remaining 80%.
- Treat candidates equally, fairly, and respectfully.
- Try to rate each candidate immediately after the interview, when the discussion is still fresh in your memory.
- Do not ask discriminating questions …
- *…about the candidate's age.*
- *…about race or ethnicity, religion, etc…*

Here again, do not hesitate to contact your local Small Business Administration office, and/or the Department of

Labor for additional information.

5.4 THE EMPLOYEE PERFORMANCE EVALUATION

At least once a year, you should evaluate each employee in your department to determine his/her trend and compare it with previously established ones. It is a time-consuming process, and if you have the possibility to outsource it, do it. You will save time, and it will improve your relationship with your personnel. Several consulting agencies can conduct these evaluations. As mentioned above, taking the time to evaluate employees will prevent discussions with your personnel. Another advantage of outsourcing it is that most of them compare not only your employees within your department, but also with the industry average.

Anyway, if you have to conduct these evaluations yourself, below are a few questions you should include in your survey.

A good evaluation starts with the review of objectives, then goes on with the right questions. I use 24 questions related to work performance and personal behavior. Each question receives a rating from 0 to 3, with 3 being the best score.
I use an Excel spreadsheet that shows on the top right, the trend of the employee on work performance and behavior. See Figure 5-1. This Excel spreadsheet can be downloaded for a small fee from www.FirstAutomobileConsultants.com

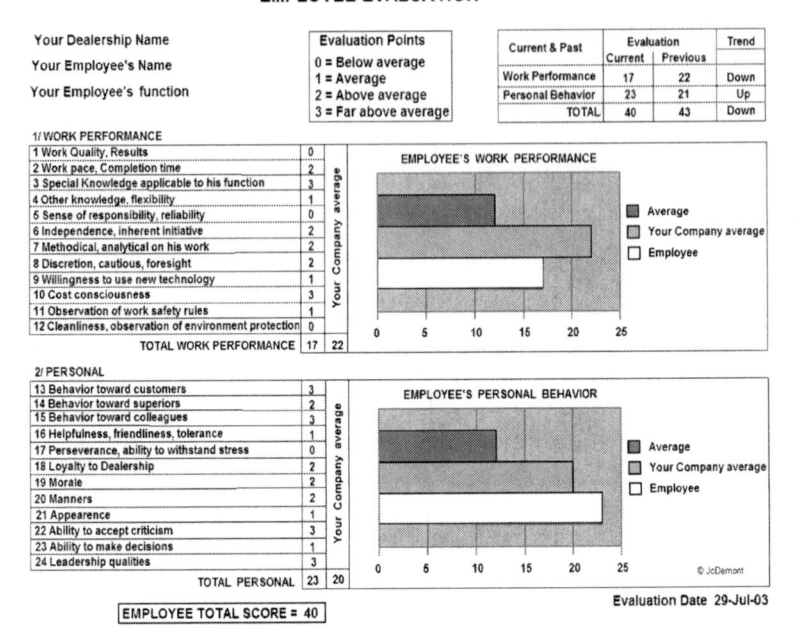

FIGURE 5-1 Employee evaluation form.

5.5 THE EMPLOYEE SATISFACTION INDEX

Everyone talks about customer satisfaction, but few about employee satisfaction. As we will discuss in the next chapter, the hierarchy of needs applies here also, and dissatisfaction seems to be more motivating than satisfaction. In a simple way, people often react more immediately to pain than to a pleasant action.

As service director/manager, you must retain your employees to keep your training expenses low, increase dealership reputation by reducing the turnover, and increase customer satisfaction and shop efficiency. You know better than everybody else how difficult and costly it is to find a competent and well-behaved technician, that you want to keep him and monitor his satisfaction with your company. Here again, it is a time-consuming process, and if you have the possibility to outsource it, do it.

Anyway, if you have to conduct these evaluations yourself, below are a few questions you must put in your survey. Ask your employees to rate each question from 1 to 5, with 5 being the best. I use only 23 questions divided in 6 sections:

4 questions on the company:

- Do you regularly receive information on the company objectives?
- Are you satisfied with the working schedule and/or working hours?
- Are employee performance evaluations fair and appropriate?
- Is the company focused on its customer's needs?

3 questions on their compensation:

- Do you feel that you are paid fairly for the job you do?
- Are you satisfied with your benefit package?
- Are your benefits comparable to other similar organizations?

4 questions on the facility:

- Is the facility well organized?
- Is the facility clean?
- Does the facility offer a safe working environment?
- Is the facility adequate to the work you perform?

4 questions on their leadership:

- Is your manager fair?
- Is your manager available when you need him/her?
- Does your manager praise you when you do a good job?
- Is your manager a good leader?

4 questions on the position:

- Do you have a good understanding of your duties & responsibilities?
- Do you receive the training you need to perform your job?
- Do you have at your disposal all special tools needed?
- Do you find this position challenging?

4 questions on teamwork:

- Do your co-workers have a teamwork attitude?
- Is your team leader well trained?
- Is the work evenly distributed?
- Do you feel that you have adequate freedom to do your job?

For a minimal fee you can download from www.FirstAutomobileConsultants.com the Excel spreadsheet that includes individual survey forms as well as all you need to prepare your employee satisfaction analysis.

Chapter 6

UNDERSTANDING YOUR CUSTOMERS

The purpose of this chapter is simple: to make your business more profitable by being able to offer your customers what they want, and when they want it. The better you understand your customers, the more responsive you can be to their needs.

You probably have heard, read, or seen in old movies some adages regarding the importance of customers. Here are some of them:

- If you think that the customer is wrong, think again!
- If you don't take care of your customers, someone else will!
- The customer is king!
- It takes years to gain one customer, and a few seconds to lose one!

And the list is almost endless.

Without customers, your business will not exist. But are these old adages still valid today? You bet they are, and particularly in the automotive service field, where we find a strong competition, as discussed in Chapter 4, *Know Your Competition.*

Customers' needs change over time. Of course, your customers still want the best Quality/Price ratio, but today's speed of life puts an emphasis on time. So, time becomes a very important factor. Customers expect you to be conveniently located and offer alternative transportation. They also expect you to offer extended working hours and to find you open when their workday is over. They expect you to offer services on weekends, when they are available; they expect you to offer a comfortable lounge with wireless high speed Internet access where they can work on their laptops while their car is being repaired. If they spend a couple of hours in the lounge, they expect you to provide some sort of drinks, coffee, etc. In this time of talking computers, they expect to find live people to talk to. Remember that you have competition!

But first, let's take a look at Maslow's pyramid for a review of the human basic needs. See Figure 6-1.

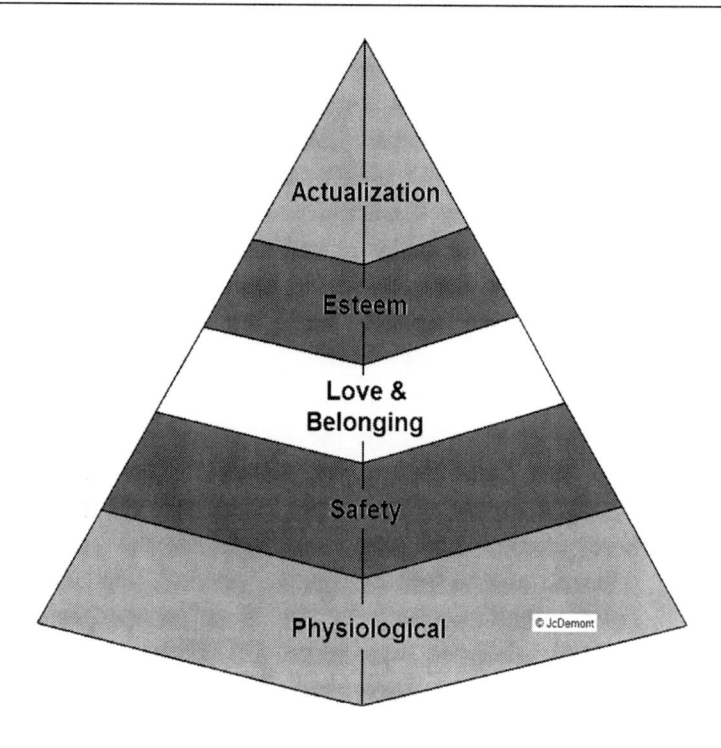

FIGURE 6-1 Maslow's pyramid.

Do you remember who Mr. Maslow is? Abraham Maslow was born April 1, 1908 in Brooklyn, New York, and was a psychologist well known for his theory of human motivation. His theory contends that as humans meet "basic needs," they seek to satisfy successively "higher needs" that occupy a set hierarchy.

- *The physiological needs.* These include the needs we have to breathe, to eat, to sleep, and to be active. In our field, there is not much we can do at this level!

- *The safety and security needs.* When the physiological needs are taken care of, this second layer of needs comes into play, and includes the needs we have for safety, stability, and protection. Here, as service department employees, we have a role to play by offering our customers a warranty for the work done, by doing the work right the first time, by keeping our word on repair costs and delays, by offering them a well-organized service department, and so on…

- *The love and belonging needs.* When the two previous layers of needs are taken care of, the third layer comes into play, and includes the need for friends, and relationships in general. As service people, and particularly the frontline people like service advisors, we must fill these customers' needs by being courteous, friendly, and making customers feel at home.

- *The esteem needs.* The next level includes the need for respect (self-respect and respect of others) and status. Here again, as service people, we have a role to play, by showing respect to customers, and showing respect to their car! By offering alternative transportation, by calling customers by their names, by offering a comfortable and well-equipped lounge, etc.

All four levels are called deficit needs. For the fifth and highest level, Maslow has used a variety of terms to refer to it: "growth motivation, being needs, and self-actualization."

- *Self-actualization* is the fifth level of Maslow's

pyramid, and it includes the continuous need to fulfill potential. Maslow pointed out at one point that only about two percent of the world's population are part of this level. So, as service people, what can we do? Respect, respect, and respect.

Keep in mind that before all, customers are humans, and the best source for you to learn about your customers is your personal interaction with them. People talk and reveal their attitudes and motivations. Listen to your customers!

To put this in a more concrete form, put yourself in a customer's shoes, and ask yourself:

- Do you know your customers well?
- Are your business clients locked into long-term relationships?
- Is your customer service excellent?
- Does your staff always have the right information when they speak to customers?
- Are customers attended quickly (not kept waiting)?
- Are customer calls answered immediately (not put on hold)?
- Is the response time for phone, fax, and e-mail inquiries acceptable?
- Is your Customer Satisfaction Index (CSI) near or at 100?
- Is your Customer Retention Rate satisfactory?
- Do you get many customer referrals?
- Are you satisfied with your Labor Sales?
- Are you satisfied with your revenue by RO?

If the answer to a number of questions is yes, it could mean that you are already providing excellent customer service. However, even with years of accumulated knowledge, there's always room for improvement. Customer needs change over time, and technology is making it easier to find out more about customers. Make sure that everyone in your organization can use this information.

If the answer to a number of these questions is no, then you should consider how you can make your business more responsive to your customers' needs, including a comprehensive Customer Relationship Management (CRM) system to help improve the understanding of your customers.

Discussing CRM systems is beyond the scope of this chapter, but as part of a move to improve customer service and sales, many businesses invest in a CRM system. CRM brings information, such as customer data, sales patterns, marketing data, and future trends, together with the aim of identifying new sales opportunities, delivering improved customer service, or offering personalized services and deals.

In addition to improving sales and profitability, CRM is reckoned to be very effective in handling customer complaints and can have a tremendous effect on your reputation.

CRM solutions fall into one of four broad categories:

- Outsourced solutions - where application service providers offer Web-based CRM solutions.
- Off-the-shelf solutions - where software companies

like Microsoft, SAP, Sales Logix, etc. offer CRM applications that integrate with existing packages. Cut-down versions of such software may be more suitable for small businesses.

- Personalized software - where consultants and software engineers will customize or create a CRM system and integrate it with your existing software. However, this can be expensive and time consuming.
- Managed solutions - these are halfway between outsourced and personalized; managed CRM involves renting a customized suite of CRM applications.

Chapter 7

TRAINING NEEDS EVALUATION

Training is a very important aspect of your success in the process of servicing your customers' cars "right the first time, every time."

Training costs your department and company a lot of money.

Training courses are expensive and most of the time out of your area/town. You have to pay for the course, for the trip and lodging.

During these training sessions, you pay your employees, but they are not physically in your shop, and are not productive.

Too often, your employees are trained with the available training courses offered by several sources, and when questioned after the course prove to have not learned anything new.

Of course, training is very important, but only when it brings a better quality of work to your dealership, and when it improves your shop's efficiency. In order to achieve this goal, your employees may need training on what they need to perform a better work quality and what is needed for them to become more efficient. Nobody knows your employees better than you do. It is your responsibility to evaluate their needs in training. But where do you start?

My method is probably not the only one or the best one out there, but I have used it for many years, and I have consequently achieved good results with it. For the purpose of this chapter, I will use one training course example, but you can use as many as are offered by the manufacturer you represent or other training sources in your area. Request each course credit (length of training course time in hours) from the manufacturer or other training sources.

Start by preparing a Microsoft Excel™ worksheet, on which the title displays the training course name and/or reference. On the same line, in the most right available cell, record the course credit given by the training provider. Below this line, create a chart where the left most column has the employee's name and/or code, then write the basics requirements for the position, and convert them into questions that will become column headers on the worksheet. Answer each question honestly by "YES" or "NO" for each employee working in that position. If you have to answer "NO" to a question, you know that the corresponding employee needs this training course. See Figure 7-1.

TRAINING NEEDS EVALUATION

1/ BASIC TECHNICAL TRAINING (SERVICE, FAC15)   Course Credit (Hour)   12.00

If one of the answers below is "NO", then the technician needs a Basic Training FAC15 !

TECHNICIAN NAME	Does your Technician have a general product knowledge?	Does your Technician know how to use & understand the Service literature?	Does your Technician know the on-board diagnostic system?	Does your Technician use the latest test appliance & special tools?	Does your Technician perform technical maintenance & inspection service?
4 Dupont	YES	YES	YES	YES	YES
6 Solver	YES	YES	NO	YES	NO
9 Rancho	YES	YES	YES	YES	YES
12 Plat	YES	YES	YES	YES	YES
16 Firon	YES	YES	YES	YES	YES
17 Mc. Donald	YES	YES	YES	YES	YES
19 Silvero	YES	YES	YES	YES	YES
20 Radina	YES	YES	YES	YES	YES
22 Samper	YES	YES	YES	YES	YES
24 Cleon	YES	YES	YES	YES	NO
29 Dollin	YES	YES	YES	YES	YES
	YES / NO	YES / NO	YES / NO	YES / NO	YES / NO
	YES / NO	YES / NO	YES / NO	YES / NO	YES / NO
	YES / NO	YES / NO	YES / NO	YES / NO	YES / NO
© JcDemont	YES / NO	YES / NO	YES / NO	YES / NO	YES / NO
2	<<Total of Employees with at least <u>one</u> "NO'				

FIGURE 7-1 Training needs evaluation worksheet.

Create a similar worksheet for each available training course. When you are finished, create a summary worksheet (see Figure 7-2), with a column for each course previously created, and link it to them. By linking to the previous worksheets, you will save a tremendous amount of time and reduce the chances for errors.

Each column should display 4 rows:

- The top one displays the course reference.
- The second one, the number of employees required to take that course.
- The third one, the total training hours (number of employees X course credit).

- And the last one, the course credit.

TRAINING NEEDS EVALUATION

16/ TRAINING NEEDS SUMMARY

| DEALERSHIP: | DATE: 5/10/2006 |

| Service Director/Manager Name: | Service Director/Manager Signature: |

Below, are the trainings needed by your Service Department:

TRAINING COURSE REFERENCE															Total Employees
FAC1 5	FAC 16	FAC 17	FAC 25	FAC 26	FAC 35	FAC 36	FAC 45	FAC 46	FAC 55	FAC 56	FAC 65	FAC 66	FAC 75	FAC 76	
2	0	0	0	0	0	0	0	0	0	0	0	0	0	0	2
24.00	0.00	0.00	0.00	0.00	0.00	0.00	0.00	0.00	0.00	0.00	0.00	0.00	0.00	0.00	Total estimated Hours 24.00
12.00	16.00	24.00	24.00	24.00	16.00	24.00	24.00	16.00	32.00	32.00	16.00	12.00	24.00	24.00	Course Credit

NOTE : Please report in the above appropriate columns the total of each of the 15 sheets. © JcDemont

FIGURE 7-2 Training needs evaluation summary.

- You now have the training needs for the entire department on one sheet.
- Your first step is to evaluate which employees you will keep and/or you will train, and which employees you will let go and/or who will not receive any training.
- Next, you will create a training needs plan based on three levels of priorities (short-term or next 12 months, medium-term or next 3 years, and long-term or over 3 years), and enter in each one the name of the employees you plan to send to training.
- Research the training availability from your sources, and from there, draw an annual training plan (not on a dry-erase board on your office wall!). Training should disturb your activity the least

possible. You must make sure that you do not send two key employees on the same dates. Don't laugh... I have seen a service manager who set vacations and training periods on a dry-erase board in his office, and who sent two Service Advisors (out of six) on vacation during the same period!

- Finally, make sure you remind your employees of their next training dates on several occasions. You do not want them to miss any planned training course; you will look unprofessional to the provider, and it will be difficult for you to book future training courses with that same provider. Some training providers even charge a no-show fee!

Be consistent with training, and conduct a training needs evaluation at least once a year to include newly hired employees, as well as to make sure the ones who have received training since your last evaluation have grabbed something from the courses!

A Microsoft Excel™ spreadsheet template called "Training Needs Evaluation" can be downloaded from www.FirstAutomobileConsultants.com for a small fee.

Chapter 8

PAY PLANS

8.1 WHY A PAY PLAN?

A pay plan is a management tool that enables you to control personnel cost, that increases employee morale, and that reduces workforce turnover. A formal pay plan provides a means of rewarding employees for their contributions to the success of your company, while ensuring that your organization receives a fair return on its investment in employee's pay.

I know that some of you are reluctant to have pay plans based on employees' performance, but when the key goals are in accordance with your company's objectives, they are excellent tools to increase your organization's profits, retain your most efficient employees, improve your relationship with the manufacturer, and improve work quality and customer satisfaction.

Pay plans don't need to be complicated. In fact, the more

elaborate the plan is, the more difficult it is to put into practice, communicate, and carry out. Pay plans should be flexible and easily adaptable to new situations found in your business. So, you want to have your pay plans oriented toward profits, manufacturer and customer satisfaction. Your plans should include incentives, and reward your employees for achieving key goals aligned with your organization's business objectives.

To be successful, pay plans should be in tune with time; you should review them at least once a year according to your company's needs and growth. Make adjustments where necessary and don't forget to retrain supervisory personnel. This is not a plan that can be established, then put aside and forgotten!

In one dealership, I found a service manager whose pay plan was written 5 years ago, when the dealership was selling about 1,200 cars per year. The service manager's pay plan had a base salary of $1,000/month, 2.5% commission on the Labor Gross Profit, and 1% commission on the operating profit.

At the time the pay plan was written, the Labor G.P. was around $170,000 per month, and the operating profit about $40,000/month. The service manager's monthly pay was about $5,650.00 ($1,000 base salary + $4,250 commission on G.P. + $400 commission on operating profit) which is considered to be a good salary.

Today, this dealer sells over 300 cars per month; the monthly Labor G.P. went up to $500,000, and the operating profit is as high as $140,000! The actual service manager's monthly pay is $14,900.00 ($1,000 + $12,500 + $1,400).

The company now faces a dilemma: considering the fact that he has been working with the company for ten years, should the service manager's pay be reduced to a more acceptable range, thus risking losing or discouraging him, or should his salary be left as is? In this particular case, if the dealership has modified the pay plan on a yearly basis according to the company's growth by reducing the percentage of the commission on Labor G.P. and operating profit, the service manager's pay will be within an acceptable range today.

On the other hand, when evaluating your technicians' hourly wages, keep in mind what Labor G.P. you want to achieve. In several service departments, I found technicians receiving 40% of the posted Labor Rate. How can these dealerships achieve 75% on Labor Gross Profit, if they already give 40% to their technicians?

A good pay plan should reward the employee for his/her team performance, and should include incentives on:

- Work quality
- Customer satisfaction
- Add-on sales (labor, parts, and accessories)
- Warranty expenses
- Labor Gross Profit
- Operating Profit

8.2 THE SERVICE DIRECTOR/MANAGER

This is the person in charge of the service department, who is responsible for profits, customer satisfaction, employee satisfaction, work quality, and warranty expenses. His plan should include incentives based on the following criteria:

- Work quality, customer satisfaction, warranty expenses, labor G.P., and operating profit of the entire service department.

8.3 THE SERVICE ADVISOR

This is the person in charge of "selling" to customers, but also, depending on your internal organization, he is the "leader" of the team(s). His plan should include incentives based on the following criteria:

- Work quality, customer satisfaction, warranty expenses, add-on sales, and the labor G.P. of the team(s).

8.4 THE SHOP FOREMAN and/or TEAM LEADER

This is the person in charge of quality and efficiency. His plan should include incentives based on the following criteria:

- Work quality, customer satisfaction, warranty expense, and labor G.P. of the team(s).

8.5 THE BOOKER

This is the person in charge of billing. His plan should include incentives based on the following criteria:

- Customer satisfaction, warranty expenses, labor G.P.

8.6 THE TECHNICIAN

This is the person who conducts the repairs. His plan should include incentives based on the following criteria:

- Customer satisfaction, warranty expenses, and labor G.P.

8.7 THE OTHER EMPLOYEES

Their pay plans should include incentives at least based on customer satisfaction, and whenever possible on the direct outcome of their work.

So far it sounds good, but how do we put this to practice? The easiest way is to prepare a matrix based on the above criteria, as well as yours. Keep in mind that you have competitors when you are preparing the matrix. You want to be in the same salary range. Let's take a look at a matrix based on a base salary and incentives based on the above criteria.

8.8 BASE SALARY:

- A low base salary with a highly rewarding incentive program will encourage productive employees to join your work force, and will push the lazy ones away. This is exactly what you want! The very best!

- A low base salary with a highly rewarding incentive program will help your company spend its payroll money wisely, and will increase its profits.
- So, go for a low base salary, but make sure that incentives are attainable, and that when associated with the base salary, they offer your employees a salary package that matches your competitors'.

8.9 WORK QUALITY:

- Count the total number of comebacks from the previous week or month, depending on the volume of your service department; use it in service director/manager pay plans.
- Count the number of comebacks during the same period, per service advisor, team leader, etc; use them in their pay plans.
- Your comebacks should be below 1%.

8.10 CUSTOMER SATISFACTION:

- Usually, your manufacturer provides you with your overall Customer Satisfaction Index, as well as the index per service advisor, team, and technician. Use these indexes in the employee pay plans.
- If your manufacturer does not provide you with the index, a consulting agency can help you. Generally, a list of customers who have visited your service department and their phone numbers is provided to the consulting agency, which then contacts your customers and later provide you with the Customer Satisfaction Index.

- Your ultimate goal should be 100% of satisfied customers.

8.11   ADD-ON SALES:

- You have several items that you want your service advisors to sell to customers, going from maintenance programs, extended warranties, accessories, to car detailing. You have to give your service advisors incentives for the sale of these products, and the simplest way is a "spiff" per item. The spiff is based on the sale price of the item and your urgency to sell it. Usually it is calculated as a percentage of the item, but presented as a rounded value (i.e. for a $430.00 alarm installed X 10% = $43.00. The presented spiff value will be $40.00).

8.12   WARRANTY EXPENSES:

- Car manufacturers monitor your warranty expenses closely, and provide you with your overall Warranty Expenses Index. This index is based on how your expenses compare to their average expenses by vehicle type and/or model, as well as how they compare with other dealers nationwide and in your area. Managing your warranty expenses by keeping them below the national and area average will prevent you from being audited by the manufacturer. Also use this index for the employee pay plans.
- Your goal should be below the national and regional average.

8.13 LABOR GROSS PROFIT:

- A nice bottom line starts with a good Labor Gross Profit. As a service director/ manager or advisor, you must focus on Labor Gross Profit. You will not be able to compensate for a few percentage points lost on G.P. with a tight expenses management! Use the percentage of G.P. versus labor sales for the employee pay plans.
- Your Labor Gross Profit objective should be 75% and above.

8.14 OPERATING PROFIT:

- One of the service director/manager's responsibilities is to make the service department profitable, and the operating profit is the bottom line. To do so, each expense must be limited to its minimum, but necessary expenses must not be cut to improve profits. For example, cutting special tools purchasing or training expenses will improve the short-term operating profit, but jeopardize it in the long run. A decrease in shop efficiency and customer satisfaction will follow. Look at your financial statements; you have many accounts you can improve. Don't be too greedy. Think about tomorrow!
- The incentive given on the operating profit should be below 1%, but attractive enough to motivate the service director/manager.

Now let's recap who gets what:

- Base salary: every position.
- Incentive on work quality: every position involved directly or indirectly with repairs and management (service director/manager; shop foreman; service advisor; team leader; and technician).
- Incentive on customer satisfaction: every position.
- Incentive on add-on sales: service advisor position.
- Incentive on warranty expenses: every position involved with management, repairs and billing (service director/manager; shop foreman; service advisor; booker; team leader; and technician).
- Incentive on Labor Gross Profit: management and service advisor positions (service director/manager; shop foreman; service advisor; booker; team leader; and technician).
- Incentive on operating profit: only top service department management (service director/manager).

Figure 8-1 shows a matrix sample for incentives evaluation on:

- Work quality, based on the percentage of comebacks.
- Customer satisfaction based on the CSI.
- Gross Profit based on the percentage of G.P.

These numbers can differ from one metro area to another, and are not applicable in some countries where employees are paid a fixed salary. But remember; use incentive pay plans whenever possible, and your customers and your bottom line will thank you!

WORK QUALITY BASED ON % OF COMEBACKS (based on the employee position, use Overall or Team Index)

Comebacks Index (rate)	<0.50 %	>0.51 % & <0.80 %	>0.81 % & <1.00 %	>1.01 % & <1.20 %	>1.21 % & <1.40 %	>1.41 % & <1.60 %	>1.61 % & <1.80 %	>1.81 % & <2.00 %	
Coefficient	1.00	0.80	0.65	0.55	0.50	0.45	0.40	0.30	There is no incentive when the percentage of Comebacks is above 2.00%!
Service Director/Manager	$600	$480	$312	$172	$86	$39	$15	$5	
Service Advisor	$600	$480	$312	$172	$86	$39	$15	$5	
Shop Foreman	$600	$480	$312	$172	$86	$39	$15	$5	
Booker	$500	$400	$260	$143	$72	$32	$13	$4	
Team Leader	$2.00	$1.60	$1.04	$0.57	$0.29	$0.13	$0.05	$0.02	For the employees paid by the hour, an hourly pay increase of X $ is given when the Index is 2.00% and above.
Technician	$2.00	$1.60	$1.04	$0.57	$0.29	$0.13	$0.05	$0.02	
Other employees	$2.00	$1.60	$1.04	$0.57	$0.29	$0.13	$0.05	$0.02	

CUSTOMER SATISFACTION INDEX (based on the employee position, use Overall or Team CSI)

Customer satisfaction index (rate)	100%	99%	98%	97%	96%	95%	94%	
Coefficient	1.00	0.80	0.65	0.55	0.50	0.40	0.00	There is no incentive when customer satisfaction index is 94% or less!
Service Director/Manager	$600	$480	$312	$172	$86	$34	$0	
Service Advisor	$600	$480	$312	$172	$86	$34	$0	
Shop Foreman	$600	$480	$312	$172	$86	$34	$0	
Booker	$500	$400	$260	$143	$72	$29	$0	
Team Leader	$2.00	$1.60	$1.04	$0.57	$0.29	$0.11	$0.00	For the employees paid by the hour, an hourly pay increase of X $ is given when the CSI is 95% and above.
Technician	$2.00	$1.60	$1.04	$0.57	$0.29	$0.11	$0.00	
Other employees	$2.00	$1.60	$1.04	$0.57	$0.29	$0.11	$0.00	

GROSS PROFIT (based on the employee position, use Overall, Team or Personal G.P.)

Labor Gross Profit Rate	78%	77%	76%	75%	74%	73%	72%	71%	
Coefficient	1.00	0.80	0.65	0.55	0.50	0.45	0.40	0.30	There is no incentive when the Gross Profit is less than 71%!
Service Director/Manager	1.00%	0.80%	0.65%	0.55%	0.50%	0.45%	0.40%	0.30%	
Service Advisor	1.00%	0.80%	0.65%	0.55%	0.50%	0.45%	0.40%	0.30%	
Shop Foreman	1.00%	0.80%	0.65%	0.55%	0.50%	0.45%	0.40%	0.30%	
Booker	1.00%	0.80%	0.65%	0.55%	0.50%	0.45%	0.40%	0.30%	© JcDemont
Team Leader	$2.00	$1.60	$1.04	$0.57	$0.29	$0.13	$0.05	$0.02	For the employees paid by the hour, an hourly pay increase of X $ is given when the G.P. is 71% and above.
Technician	$2.00	$1.60	$1.04	$0.57	$0.29	$0.13	$0.05	$0.02	
Other employees	$2.00	$1.60	$1.04	$0.57	$0.29	$0.13	$0.05	$0.02	

FIGURE 8-1 Matrix sample for incentives evaluation.

Chapter 9

THE SERVICE CYCLE ANALYSIS

The *Service Cycle Analysis* is probably one of the best tools you have as a service director/manager to improve customer satisfaction and shop efficiency. In order to accomplish this, you should evaluate each of the steps your customer has to go through. It takes time but you must do it at least twice a year.

We recommend that you contact an external source like a consulting agency to conduct such analysis. They will assess your service department without any biases, and will identify some points that you won't be able to because you are at the dealership every day, and you are accustomed to them.

We call this analysis the *Service **CYCLE** Analysis*, because each one of the 7 steps your customers go through creates a cycle. See Figure 9-1.

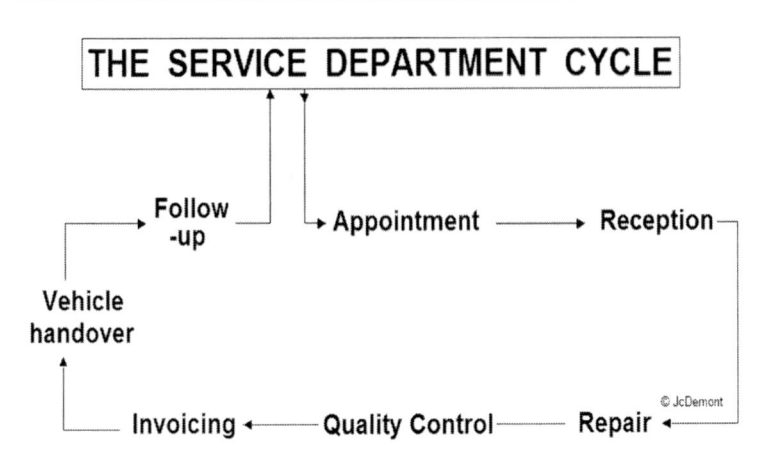

FIGURE 9-1 The seven steps of the service cycle analysis.

9.1 APPOINTMENT

When conducting this analysis, you start by the fist step your customers go through when dealing with your service department, which is the appointment.

Put yourself in the customer's shoes and call your appointment desk from a private phone:

- Was the line busy?
- How many times did the phone ring before someone answered?
- Did the person who answered the phone give the company's name?
- Did the person mention that you had reached the service department?
- Did the person introduce himself/herself?
- Was he/she polite and courteous?
- Was the communication clear of background noises?

- Were your name and telephone number requested?
- Were your vehicle brand, model, and year requested?
- Was the repair needed requested by the appointment coordinator?
- Were you given a price range?
- Were you given an immobilization time?
- Was the appointment date less than a week from the time you called?
- Was an alternative transportation discussed?

This is the first contact your customers will have with your service department; so, they expect a pleasant experience over the phone. First, the line should not be busy. Then, your receptionist must answer the phone before the third ring. Then, he/she should give the company's name, the department you have reached, his/her name and title, and a short welcome phrase. There should not be any audible background noises. He/she must request your name, as well as your telephone number and your vehicle brand and/or model. He/she must ask you what needs to be done for the vehicle, and should give you the necessary immobilization time for the repair, and a price range. The appointment date should not be more than one week from the time of call. The alternative transportation should be provided to you (shuttle, loaner, car rental, etc.) if available at your company.

Once you have found the answers to these questions, put them down on a sheet of paper, and draw a list of strengths and a list of weaknesses. See Figure 9-2. Then write at the bottom the idea(s) you think will solve the problem.

1. Appointment ~ Results

• *Strengths*

* Qualified and well trained staff.

* Computerized appointment system (ADP).

* WEB based appointment system available.

• *Weaknesses*

* Difficulty to obtain an appointment by phone (Dealership lines always busy).

© JcDemont

Installation of a direct line for appointments only!

FIGURE 9-2 Summary of strengths and weaknesses. Here for the appointment step.

9.2 SERVICE DRIVE/RECEPTION

So far, your customer has an idea of your dealership's service department based on his/her experience over the phone. It is very important that the service drive and reception be a pleasant experience that meets the customers' expectations from the first contact. You should make sure that:

- The signage directs a new customer directly to the right place.
- The service drive/reception area is clear of vehicles as much as possible.

- The service drive/reception area is clean and well organized.
- Depending on the system you use, porters and/or service advisors are well groomed and have a professional appearance and attitude.
- Whoever is in charge should show customers respect and protect his/her investment by placing seat and steering wheel covers and floor mat protectors in front of the customer.
- The waiting time to sit with a service advisor is less than five minutes.
- The service advisor's desk is well organized and clean.
- Specials are displayed at the service advisor's desk.
- Service advisors are friendly to the customers.
- The right amount of time is spent with customers.
- The customer's waiting area is clean and tidied.
- The lounge meets today's customer's expectation.

A picture is worth a thousand words! So take some pictures of the service drive/reception, and customers' lounge from a customer's standpoint. Then, evaluate the average time customers wait to sit with an advisor; this should not exceed five minutes if your appointment coordinators set proper appointment times. Observe and listen to conversations between service advisors and their customers; you can pinpoint weaknesses in your system when, for example, several customers ask the same questions. Make sure your service advisors don't "shoot" the customer; they need to spend some time to propose services, accessories, etc. Make sure the lounge offers at least what your competitors offer: coffee, donuts, wireless Internet access, etc.

When you find answers to these questions, put them down on a sheet of paper, and draw a list of strengths and weaknesses that is similar to the one you did for the previous stages. On the opposite page, insert your pictures.

9.3 REPAIRS

Your customers don't have access to your workshop. You probably don't see the necessity in having a nice, clean, and well-organized shop. A well-organized shop will increase the efficiency, as well as the technicians' desire to work for you. A well-organized shop will decrease the risk of damaged vehicles during repairs and the risk of work accidents. So make sure that:

- Your shop is clean from oil, grease, and dirt.
- Used parts are properly stored and put away.
- Special tools are clean and put back on the racks after each use.
- Workbenches are free of boxes, used parts, etc.
- Each technician has a designated area.
- Each work stall is marked on the floor.
- Technicians use special tools and equipment adequately.
- Technicians respect customers' cars.
- Technicians do not gather at the back counter to socialize.

Even if you think that everything looks neat, you should take a few pictures of the shop, its benches, its back counter, and of the tools' room like you did for the reception area. You will be amazed at the number of things you failed to notice during your walk-around. Then, think about safety: if oil, grease, coolant, used parts, boxes, etc. are spread on the floor, not only will your shop pollute, but this might be the cause of serious problems with the Environment Protection Agency. By failing to keep a safe environment, you are also increasing the risks of clashes among your employees. Make sure that everything is stored in appropriate containers, and at the proper location. In the tools room and/or on the tools racks, special tools must be in working condition, clean and ready to use. The workbenches must be free for your technicians to be able to work on them. By designating an area for each technician, not only are you preventing problems from arising between technicians, but also you give each of them a sense of responsibility as they must maintain and organize their area. As a professional, when walking through the shop, look to see if your technicians are working with special tools, if they tighten wheels with torque wrenches, etc. Verify that your technicians respect the customers' cars by installing fender covers, by working gently and professionally. Also take a look at the back counter; it should be clear of warranty parts and technicians.

Here again, when you have answered these questions, put them down on a sheet of paper, and draw a list of strengths and weaknesses as you previously did. On the opposite page, insert your pictures.

9.4 QUALITY CONTROL

Your goal is to reach the ultimate 100% customer satisfaction, and it cannot be done without a quality control system. Regardless of the quality control in place at your dealership, as a service manager, you have to make sure it works effectively. Below are some points you must consider looking at for reference:

- Who is in charge and responsible for quality control?
- Is the quality control sheet used, and stapled to the work order?
- Does this employee have enough credibility and power to impose a touch-up?
- What is part of the control?
- What is the percentage of controlled vehicles?

Your time is precious, and the easiest and quickest way to make sure your quality control system works is to go to the park, take a car ready for delivery, request the Repair Order from the cashier, then go over the quality control sheet, and test drive the vehicle around the block. Then, compare your findings with what your quality control report indicates. Also, ask the cashier for 10 or 20 ROs for which customers have already been called, and count how many QC sheets are attached; then do the math to figure out the percentage of controlled cars.

Here again, when you have answered these questions, put them down on a sheet of paper, and draw a list of strengths and weaknesses as you did for the previous stages.

9.5 INVOICING

The invoice should be ready prior to the customer's arrival. The invoice must wait for the customer, not the other way around. The invoice is your business card. Make sure it is clean and well written, and contains updated information. You should be able to answer the following questions:

- Is the invoice ready prior to customer arrival?
- Is the invoice clean and well presented?
- Does the undertaken work match the customer's requests?
- Are labor codes present?
- Does the total amount match the estimate?
- Is the Repair Warranty policy displayed on the invoice?
- Is the name of the service advisor on the invoice?
- Is the thank-you note present?
- Is there a list of additional needed work?

Here again, when you have answered these questions, put them down on a sheet of paper, and draw a list of strengths and weaknesses as you did for the previous stages.

9.6 VEHICLE HANDOVER

Now, the customer is here to pick up his/her vehicle. Remember that his/her time is as precious as yours is. Don't make him/her wait!

- Has the service advisor "sold" the invoice to the customer?
- Was there a line of customers waiting to pay their invoices at the cashier's window?
- As soon as the customer paid, did the cashier call for the vehicle?
- Has the customer been waiting for his/her car more than two minutes?

- Was the car clean on both the inside and the outside?
- Was your service advisor and/or porter courteous?
- Did the person who delivered the vehicle remove the seat cover, the floor mat, and the steering wheel cover in front of the customer?
- Was the handover area clean and well organized?

Here again, once you have answered all the questions, put them down on a sheet of paper, and draw a list of strengths and weaknesses like you did for the previous stages.

9.7 FOLLOW-UP

The customer paid his/her invoice, took his/her vehicle, seemed happy, and did not complain about anything! So you are off the hook for this time, right?

Not just yet! As you know, one unhappy customer will share his/her bad experience with friends, relatives, coworkers, neighbors, and at least 13 people will now know how bad your service is. When happy, the customer will share his/her good experience with only a few persons. You do not want your customers to spread a bad image about your shop, nor do you want them to give you a bad CSI when surveyed. This is the reason for which the follow-up is such an important step. Each customer must be called the week following his/her visit, and prior to the manufacturer's survey, to allow you to eventually correct mistakes if there are any. On a daily basis, take a few closed ROs (customer paid & warranty), make a list, and verify with the employee in charge of follow-ups that:

- All customers on your list have been called.
- The answers have been recorded and stored.
- The name of the employee is written on each record sheet.
- The name of the person who answered the call is written on each record sheet.
- The customer answered positively to all questions.
- Customers are satisfied with their service experience at your shop.

Here again, when you have answered these questions, put them on a sheet of paper, and draw a list of strengths and weaknesses like you did for the previous stages.

You now have in your hands pictures, strengths, and weaknesses for each stage your customer goes through when dealing with your department. Take the time to analyze each sheet and the corresponding pictures to pinpoint what can be improved at each stage.

I guarantee you that by doing this analysis twice a year, you will undoubtedly improve your customer satisfaction, as well as your bottom line. Remember that this analysis is at its best when outsourced.

Chapter 10

THE REPAIR ORDER

The Repair Order (RO) is the most important document in the service department. It is the only link between the customer and the service department. It's a contract between the two parties, so you want to make sure you do what it takes to protect your company, and it starts with the customer's approval and signature. Then, the RO becomes a management tool that gives you a pretty good picture of what is going on in your service department.

For several service directors/managers, the RO analysis is limited to seeing the customer signature, as well as the estimated amount being approved.

- What else, other than the customer's signature and his estimate approval, should the service manager look for in a RO?
- How many ROs should be analyzed?
- How often ROs should be examined?

In this chapter, we will answer these questions, and we will discuss the RO as a management tool, and the importance of its analysis.

10.1 WHAT TO LOOK FOR IN A RO?

First, you have to verify that your service advisors have all the customer's information (including updated phone numbers), and the vehicle information (including mileage, fuel level, delivery date, and date of end of warranty). Then, you need to find out if the car was at your shop in the past 90 days, and if this visit is a comeback.

You want to check that the labor codes are correct, that prices and labor times are accurate, and that your service advisors are selling needed work as well as promoting in-house specials. You want to examine the number of items written on the RO; more items per RO will increase your Average Labor Sales by RO. You also want to know the Labor Cost for each RO.

10.2 HOW MANY ROs SHOULD BE ANALYZED?

The number of ROs that should be analyzed is directly associated to the volume of work in your shop. Yet, as a rule of thumb, you should analyze at least 50% of the ROs written by each Service Advisor in order to have a clear idea of what is going on in your service department.
Thus you should examine an equal number of ROs for each service Advisor.

10.3 HOW OFTEN SHOULD ROs BE EXAMINED?

You should examine ROs on a daily, weekly, or monthly basis, depending on the volume of work in your shop.

We recommend that you use the *Daily Repair Order Analysis* showed in Figure 10-1 illustrated below to record your findings and to get a good picture of your service department.

Finally, at the end of each month, you must report these numbers on the "Monthly Repair Order Analysis," which we will discuss next.

DAILY REPAIR ORDER ANALYSIS

Service Advisor Name/#					(A)								Date:	(B)	
R.O. #	Mileage	90 days	Come -Back	One Item R.O.	Labor Sales ($)				Flat Rate Hours				Effective Labor Rate	Total Labor Cost
					1(*)	2(*)	3(*)	Total	1(*)	2(*)	3(*)	Total		
325672	145000	N	N	N	$150.00	$0.00	$200.00	$350.00	1.00	0.00	2.00	3.00	$116.67	$98.00
325672	145000	N	N	N	$138.00	$0.00	$0.00	$138.00	1.00	0.00	0.00	1.00	$138.00	$41.40
①	②	③	④	⑤	⑥	⑦	⑧	⑨	⑩	⑪	⑫	⑬	⑭	⑮
							⑯							
													© JcDemont	
TOTAL	0	0	0	$310.00	$7.00	$208.00	$497.00	12.00	11.00	14.00	17.00		26	
Percentage	0.0%	0.0%	0.0%	62.37%	1.41%	41.85%	100.00%	71%	65%	82%	100%			

Number of analyzed ROs:	⑰	Effective Labor Rate:	㉗
Number of cars in shop within 90 days:	⑱ ㉑	Avg. Labor charged /RO:	㉘
Number of Come-Back:	⑲ ㉒		
Number of One Item ROs:	⑳ ㉓	Avg. FRH charged /RO:	㉙
LABOR GROSS PROFIT:	㉔	㉕ (Must be > 70%)	

Total Labor Cost

Note on Labor Sales(*) & Flat Rate Hours (*): 1 = Competitive Labor; 2 = Maintenance; 3 = Repair

FIGURE 10-1 Daily repair order analysis worksheet.

10.4 DAILY REPAIR ORDER ANALYSIS

Let's go back to our *Daily Repair Order Analysis*. This spreadsheet indicates the service advisor's name at the top left corner, labeled (A), and at the top right corner, the date (B).

Then, it includes 15 columns, and 20 lines to analyze 20

ROs per page. Starting from the left,

- column (1) shows the *RO number*;
- column (2) shows the *mileage*;
- column (3) shows *if the car was at the shop in the last 90 days* (enter "Y" if positive, and "N" if negative);
- column (4) shows *if it is a comeback* (enter "Y" if positive, and "N" if negative);
- column (5) shows if there is only *one item on this RO* (enter "Y" if positive, and "N" if negative);
- column (6) displays the *amount of Labor Sales for Competitive Labor* (includes such items as lube, oil, and filter, alignments, balance, and tire rotation);
- column (7) displays the *amount of Labor Sales for Maintenance Labor* (which are generally recommended by the manufacturer such as brakes, tune-ups, filters, and drive belts);
- column (8) displays the *amount of Labor Sales for Repairs Labor* (includes most of those repairs that are not included in the competitive and maintenance categories);
- column (9) is the *Total of columns 6, 7, and 8;*
- column (10) displays the *Flat Rate Hours sold for Competitive Labor*;
- column (11) displays the *Flat Rate Hours sold for Maintenance Labor*;
- column (12) displays the *Flat Rate Hours sold for Repairs Labor*;
- column (13) is the *Total of columns 10, 11, and 12*;
- column (14) shows the *Effective Labor Rate for this RO*, and it is obtained by dividing the Total Labor Sales from column (9) by the Total Flat Rate Hours

sold from column (13). This is a very important indicator.

- and finally, column (15) shows the *Total Cost of Labor for this RO*. This is another very important indicator. It should be at or below your average technician pay.

The bottom of these columns (16) shows the total of each column, and the next line shows the percentage (i.e. at the bottom of column 6, it shows that $310 was charged and that the Competitive Labor Sales represents 62.37% of your Total Labor Sales).

The next line (17) counts the number of ROs, which are analyzed in column (1).

The following line (18) shows the number of cars that were at the shop in the last 90 days, and (21) the percentage they represent.

The following line (19) shows the number of comebacks, and (22) the percentage they represent.

The next line (20) shows the number of ROs with only one item, and (23) the percentage they represent.

The last line (24) shows the *Labor Gross Profit*, and (25) the percentage it represents.

At the bottom right of the page, line (26) shows the total labor cost (sum of column 15).

Line (27) shows the Effective Labor Rate for the analyzed ROs. Compare it with your Hourly Labor Rate; it should be above it. If it is below it, then look for Labor discounts, or high percentage of warranty work.

Line (28) shows the Average Labor Sales per RO. Compare it with the average in your area. If it is above the area average, chances are that you overcharge customers, and vice versa.

The last line (29) shows the average FRH charged per RO. Here again, compare it with the average in your area. If it's above the area average, chances are that you overcharge customers, and vice versa.

You are probably asking yourself: "Okay, there are a lot of lines, columns, and numbers, but what can I do with them?"

As a service director/manager, your time is precious; thus you do not want to take the time to fill out this sheet. Your secretary or a data entry clerk can complete this task daily. You want to focus on a few areas of the *Daily Repair Order Analysis*, though, in order to have a quick overview of your department. First you will look at:

The bottom of columns (6), (7), and (8) (Labor Sales):

- Line "Total" informs you of the Labor Sales on Competitive, Maintenance, and Repair.
- Line "Percentage" shows the percentage of the Labor Sales on Competitive, Maintenance, and Repair versus the Total Labor Sales. Focus on the percentage of Repairs; it should be above 45%.
- This is the first very important indicator, because it gauges your shop's performance versus that of your competitors.

For example, if the Maintenance column shows a small percentage, it means that your customers are going elsewhere for maintenance. It is the same thing for Competitive Labor and Repairs. In either case, you are losing market shares, and you must analyze your competition (Price, Convenience, Work Quality, Customer Satisfaction, etc.) and adjust your weak points accordingly. If your Labor Rate is much higher than the ones of your competitors regarding Competitive and Maintenance work, keep in mind that these jobs do not require a master technician, so you can use a low-skilled (cheaper) technician and offer a lower Labor Rate to match that of your competitors. We discuss how you can lower your Maintenance Labor Rate and keep your actual Effective Labor Rate in Chapter 11, *Effective and Variable Labor Rates.*

Next, look at the frame at the bottom of the page, and look at:

- ***Cars at shop in the last 90 days (18), and the percentage that they represent (21):***

A percentage higher than 5% can be the result of incomplete work during previous visits, parts unavailability, car damages during previous visits, hidden comebacks, etc. A good practice would be to request your shop foreman to evaluate the cause for each case.

- ***Car Comebacks (19), and the percentage that they represent (22):***

A percentage higher than 2% can indicate a work quality problem. If you have a quality control in place, review it, and if you do not have one, it is time to consider one.

- ***Number of One Item ROs (20), and the percentage that they represent (23):***

A high percentage usually indicates that your service advisors are not "up-selling." Compare the average labor charged by RO with the benchmarks provided by the manufacturer you represent, and/or by your dealer association (usually around 15%).

- ***Labor Gross Profit (24), and the percentage it represents (25):***

As a service director/manager this is the indicator you must focus on. Your goal should be 75% or above. It is not uncommon to find a well-managed shop with a GP of 75% and above.

- ***Effective Labor Rate (27):***

As a rule of thumb, your Effective Labor Rate should be within 10% of your posted Labor Rate. The service advisor is the one most responsible for achieving the desired result. If your EFL is too low, look for Labor discounts, Undersold Labor times, Menu Priced operations, Labor Rate discounted for internal works, and percentage of warranty jobs, etc.

- ***Average Labor Charged by RO (28), and Average Hours charged by RO (29):***

This is your oversold/undersold gauge. Here, the service director/manager can use several benchmarks; one can be provided by the brand manufacturer that your dealership represents, and the other by your dealer association. We recommend that you use your own benchmarks by controlling all ROs for at least three months, and making sure that the Flat Rate Hours charged on the ROs reflect the Manufacturer Suggested Times. Then develop your own benchmark. We usually find around 2.50 hours in developed countries, and up to 6 hours in some countries with bad road systems!

When the Labor or FRH by RO is higher than the benchmarks, you are overcharging your customers, and when below, undercharging them.

Running a service department profitably today has become much more of an exact science than in past years. Realizing the importance of RO analysis is definitely the basis of that science.

10.5 MONTHLY REPAIR ORDER ANALYSIS

Now, let us take a look at the *Monthly Repair Order Analysis*. This is the document on which you will report your daily sheets per service advisor at the end of the month. You should keep this document for future reference. It is quite similar to the Daily RO Analysis, but regroups all service advisors. This gives you a complete overview of your shop on a single page. See Figure 10-2.

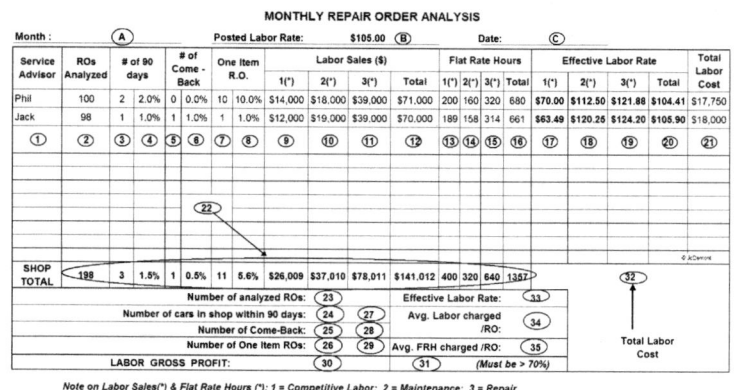

FIGURE 10-2 Monthly repair order analysis worksheet.

This spreadsheet shows on the left top (A) the Month being analyzed, at the center (B), it shows the Posted (customer paid) Labor Rate, and on the right, the Date (B).

Then, it includes 21 columns and 12 lines to analyze the ROs up to 12 service advisors. Starting from left,

- column (1) shows the *Service Advisor Name or ID*;
- column (2) shows the *Total of ROs analyzed for this S.A.;*
- column (3) shows the *Total of cars that have visited the shop in the last 90 days for this S.A.*;
- column (4) shows the *Percentage of cars that were in the shop in the last 90 days for this S.A.*;
- column (5) shows the *Total comebacks for this S.A.*;
- column (6) displays the *Percentage of comebacks for this S.A.*;
- column (7) shows the *Total of one-item ROs for this S.A.*;

- column (8) shows the *Percentage of one-item ROs for this S.A.*;
- column (9) displays the *amount of Labor Sales for Competitive Labor*;
- column (10) displays the *amount of Labor Sales for Maintenance Labor;*
- column (11) displays the *amount of Labor Sales for repairs*;
- column (12) is the *Total of columns 9, 10, and 11;*
- column (13) displays the *Flat Rate Hours sold for Competitive Labor*;
- column (14) displays the *Flat Rate Hours sold for Maintenance Labor*;
- column (15) displays the *Flat Rate Hours sold for Repairs Labor*;
- column (16) is the *Total of columns 13, 14, and 15*;
- column (17) shows the *Effective Labor Rate for Competitive Labor;*
- column (18) shows the *Effective Labor Rate for Maintenance Labor;*
- column (19) shows the *Effective Labor Rate for Repair Labor;*
- column (20) displays the *Effective Labor Rate for this S.A.;*
- column (21) shows the *Total Cost of Labor for this S.A.*

The bottom of the column (22) represents the Total of columns (2) to (16).

The next line (23) counts the Total number of ROs analyzed in column (2).

The following line (24) shows the number of cars that were at the shop in the last 90 days, and (27) the percentage they represent.

The following line (25) shows the number of comebacks, and (28) the percentage they represent.

Next line (26) shows the number of ROs with only one item, and (29) the percentage they represent.

The last line (30) the *Labor Gross Profit*, and (31) the percentage it represents.

At the bottom right of the page, the line (32) shows the total labor cost (sum of column (21)).

Line (33) shows the Effective Labor Rate for the analyzed ROs. Compare it with your Hourly Labor Rate.

Line (34) shows the Average Labor Sales per RO. Compare it with the average in your area. If it is above the area average, chances are that you overcharge customers, and vice versa.

The last line (35) shows the average FRH charged per RO. Here again, compare it with the average in your area. If it's above the area average, chances are that you overcharge customers, and vice versa.

As we previously did with the *Daily Repair Order Analysis*, you want to focus on the frame at the bottom of the page to have a quick picture of your department. We will not repeat the steps and benchmarks, since they are the same as we have already discussed on the *Daily Repair Order Analysis*.

10.6 CHAPTER SUMMARY AND CONCLUSIONS

Let's briefly summarize the most important elements of this chapter and then organize them in chronological order:

1. Conduct a Daily ROs Analysis per service advisor (at least 50% of written ROs), by using the *Daily Repair Order Analysis* sheet.
2. Look at the percentage of Labor mix (Competitive, Maintenance, and Repair).
3. Look at the percentage of cars that were at your shop in the last 90 days.
4. Look at the percentage of comebacks.
5. Look at the percentage of one-item ROs.
6. Look at the percentage of G.P.
7. Look at the Effective Labor Rate.
8. Look at the Labor and Hours charged by RO.
9. At the end of the Month, conduct the same analysis, using the *Monthly Repair Order Analysis* sheet.

Chapter 11

EFFECTIVE AND VARIABLE LABOR RATES

The *Effective Labor Rate* has significant impact on the overall gross and net profitability. It is critical to routinely monitor it. Although having a high Effective Labor Rate does not guarantee profitability, it will establish the initial condition for profit and a solid foundation to build on.

The Effective Labor Rate is obtained by dividing the Total Labor Sales by the Total Hours Sold, and should be within 10 percent of your posted Customer Rate. It is an important aspect of your profit, and must be monitored daily!

First example:

- A dealership has a posted Customer labor rate of $105.
- A Total Labor Sales of $750,000.00 for a given period.

- And a Total of 7,000 Hours sold for the same period.
- Its ELR is: $750,000.00 : 7,000 = $107.14.

Thus, this dealership is doing well; its ELR is about 2% higher than its posted labor rate. Can it do better? Probably, by frequently analyzing its Repair Orders.

Now, look at the second example:

- A dealership has a posted Customer labor rate of $105.
- A Total Labor Sales of $750,000.00 for a given period.
- And a Total of 8,000 Hours sold for the same period.
- Its ELR is: $750,000.00 : 8,000 = $93.75.

This dealership is not doing well at all; its ELR is about 11% lower than its posted labor rate.

The service director/manager in example #2 needs to identify the cause of the lower ELR by analyzing the Repair Orders for the given period.

Several factors result in a low Effective Labor Rate. Following is a list of the most common ones:

- Freebies on labor.
- Labor discounts.
- Use of a lower labor rate for internal work (pre-owned vehicles, PDI, etc.).
- High percentage of warranty works.

- Menu pricing labor.
- Work mix.

A lot of service directors/managers are reluctant to try *Variable Labor Rates pricing*, but we recommend that every service department follow the structured Variable Labor Rates pricing system. This system allows increasing customer loyalty by keeping them in the shop for competitive and maintenance works. It includes three rates:

- *Competitive Rate* includes such items as lube, oil, and filter, alignment, balance, and tire rotation.

- *Maintenance Rate* for labor operations that are generally recommended by the manufacturer such as brake, tune-up, filters, and drive belts.

- *Repair Rate* for most labor operations not included in the competitive and maintenance categories, and which usually require special equipment and highly trained technicians.

It is possible to maintain the same Effective Labor Rate, and still offer a competitive Labor Rate for competitive and maintenance works.

Look at this example:

- A dealership has a posted Customer Labor Rate of $105.
- A Total Labor Sales of $750,000.00 for a given period.
- And a Total of 7,075 Hours sold for the same period.
- The ELR for that period is $106.

- Its competitors charge $80/hour for competitive and maintenance works.
- The percentage of competitive and maintenance works performed in its shop is 10%.

Can this dealer match its competitor's rates and still keep its $106 ELR? *YES!*

The dealership will use its competitor's rate of $80/hour for competitive and maintenance works.

Here is the formula to calculate the new Labor Rate for Repair works:

New Repair labor rate =(Actual ELR *minus* (Competitor Labor Rate *multiplied by* % maintenance performed in your shop)) *divided* by the percentage of all works other than competitive and maintenance.

New Repair Labor Rate =($106.00 – ($80.00 * 10%)) / 90% (100% – 10%) = **$108.90.**

Let's verify:

Competitive and maintenance labor sales:

- 7,075 hours * 10% = 707.50 hours
- $80.00 X 707.50 = **$56,600.**

Repairs Labor Sales:

- 7,075 hours * 90% = 6,367.50 hours
- $108.90 X 6,367.50 = **$693,400.**

Total Labor Sales: $56,600.00 + $693,400.00 = **$750,000.**

Effective Labor Rate: $750,000 / (707.50 + 6367.50) = $106.

Using this pricing system is a win/win situation for you and your customers:

- Your customers pay a competitive rate (matching your competitor's rates) for competitive and maintenance works, and a fair price for other repairs that require additional equipment, greater skills, and more expensive technicians.
- You keep the same Effective Labor Rate, and increase your customer loyalty.

Unfortunately, competitive and maintenance rates are not identical. That is the reason we highly recommend a variable rate pricing, using the three different rates. Also, by offering three rates, you will be competitive in all aspects of your work mix, and this will consequently increase your labor and parts sales.

As we saw on the previous example, it is possible to offer your customers two labor rates and still keep the actual Effective Labor Rate. Now, can you offer two lower labor rates and still keep the same ELR?

YES you can! And here is the example:

- A dealership has a posted Customer labor rate of $105.
- A Total Labor Sales of $750,000.00 for a given period.

- And a Total of 7,075 Hours sold for the same period.
- The ELR for that period is $106.
- His competitors charge $70/hour for competitive works.
- His competitors charge $80/hour for maintenance works.
- The percentage of competitive works performed at his shop is 10%.
- The percentage of maintenance works performed at his shop is 15%.

New Repair labor rate = (Actual ELR *minus* ((Competitive Labor Rate *multiplied by* % of competitive work done in your shop) *plus* (Maintenance Labor Rate *multiplied by* % of maintenance work done in your shop)) *divided by* the percentage of all works other than competitive and maintenance.

New Repair labor rate =($106.00 – (($70.00 * 10%) + ($80.00 * 15%)) / 75% (100% – 25%) = $116.00.

Let's verify:

Competitive labor sales:

- 7,075 hours * 10% = 707.50 hours
- $70.00 X 707.50 = **$49,525.**

Maintenance Labor Sales:

- 7,075 hours * 15% = 1,061.25 hours
- $80.00 X 1,061.25 = **$84,900.**

Repairs Labor Sales:

- 7,075 hours * 75% = 5,306.25 hours
- $116.00 X 5,306.25 = **$615,525.**

Total Labor Sales: $49,525.00 + $84,900.00 + $615,525.00 = **$750,000.**

Effective Labor Rate: $750,000 / (707.50 + 1.061.25 + 5,306.25) = $106.

In conclusion, this is a win, win, and win situation! You have no reason to give away these market shares to your competitors, and by offering the variable rate pricing, your **customers will be happy** because:

- *You offer them the same rates that they find in other places where they are less personalized than at your dealership.*
- *You make your shop their only stop for their entire automobile needs.*

Your **parts department will be happy** because *they are going to sell more parts.*

Your **sales department will be happy** because *the improved customer loyalty will increase their sales.*

Then, the **manufacturer will be happy** because of *the increase in customer satisfaction and loyalty.*

And finally, the **dealer's principal will be happy** to see that *all this was done without any additional costs but an* *increased profit.*

So, go for it!

To save you time and money, a specific calculator can be downloaded for a minimal fee from the online catalog at www.firstautomobileconsultants.com

Chapter 12

MANAGING SHOP SUPPLIES

Shop supplies are small-cost items (bolts, nuts, pins, screws, electrical connectors, electrical tape, etc.), but put all together, they can take a big chunk of your gross profit. Shop supplies expenses need to be closely monitored, and are the service director/manager's responsibility.

On a monthly basis, you must analyze your shop supply expenses, and compare them to your sales.

Depending on the country or state you do business in, you have different options to charge shop supplies to your customers:

- If you are in a country or state that allows charging customers for shop supplies, charge what the country or state allows you to. Usually, it is based on a percentage of the Labor Sales. Some countries or states allow around 10% of the Labor Sales, with a maximum set limit.

- Example: The country/state allows 10% shop supplies charge with a limit of $50.00:
- Labor Sales invoice of $250. Shop supplies charged to the customer: $250 X 10% = $25.00.
- Labor Sales invoice of $500. Shop supplies charged to the customer: $500 X 10% = $50.00.
- Labor Sales invoice of $1500. Shop supplies: $1500 X 10% = $150.00. Since it exceeds the maximum limit, the $50 maximum allowed is charged to customer.

If you are in a country or state that does not allow charging customers for shop supplies, you must charge them as parts. Be aware that if the part is charged as a whole, you must give the customer the remaining. Example: you use only .5 liter of a given liquid, but charge the customer for 1 liter; the remaining 0.5 liter must be given back to the customer.

But, keep in mind that either way, the shop supplies expenses must be passed on to your customers. When balancing this account each month, your result should be positive, eventually equal, but never negative.

So far, we have discussed the options you have to charge shop supplies to your customers. Now, let's take a look at how they are charged to your department, and the different options you have depending on your internal organization, and how your technicians are paid.

If you are in a country or state that does not allow charging customers for shop supplies, the parts department will charge them directly to the customer's RO without your intervention.

Now, if you are in a country or state that allows to charge customers for shop supplies, you have two options:

- The first one: shop supplies are stored in the service department. An R.O. is opened at the beginning of each month. Once a week, the shop foreman updates the inventory, and the parts department will charge the service department through this RO for the supplies that were used. At the end of the month, the RO is closed. In this case, the technician takes what he needs, and won't lose any time at the parts back counter for a few cents' part, and if your technicians are paid by salary, you will save a lot.
- The second option: the shop supplies are stored in the parts department. An RO is opened at the beginning of each month. Every time a technician needs one of those items, he will have to go to the back counter, make his request, and sign the RO to get it. At the end of the month, the RO is closed, and the parts department will charge the service department for the supplies. With this option, you have a better control of the shop supplies inventory, but also a decrease in technicians and workshop's efficiencies.

Look at this example:

- You have 10 technicians making an average of $20/hour who perform services on an average of 6 cars per day. Your average Labor Sales by RO is $150, and your local institution allows you to charge a 10% shop supplies on Labor Sales:
- Your shop supplies sales are 10 X 6 = 60 X $150 = $9,000.00 X 10% = $900.00.

- The parts department charges you $700 for the supplies. Your Profit is $200.
- If your technicians have to wait only five minutes at the parts back counter to get their shop supplies, it will cost you: 10(technicians) X 6 (cars) = 60 X 5(minutes) = 5 hours X $20 = $200.

In this case, the profit you made on shop supplies ($200) is eaten by the cost of the time wasted by the technicians ($200). Do you think that $200 worth of shop supplies would be lost or stolen if the shop supplies were stored in the service department? Yet, the choice is yours, and it should be made according to your internal organization and the confidence you have in your staff.

So far, few dealerships purchase shop supplies, including paint-related items, through co-ops, and save lots of money on shop supplies. This practice becomes more and more frequent nowadays. "Leader Auto Resources" is based in Canada, but it is one of the few co-ops serving the automotive dealerships in the United States.

In conclusion, you should monitor your shop supplies expenses monthly, and compare your current expenses with historical ones to see if and where changes occur. If you also have a body shop, the necessity for managing your shop supplies tightly is even greater, because of the quantity of paint-related items used, and their costs.

Chapter 13

DISCOUNTS

Nowadays, you see discounts everywhere. Car dealerships are offering thousand-dollar discounts on new car purchases. TV, Internet, newspapers, magazines, flyers are filled with ads offering discounts. Everybody wants bargains. Smart buyers are used to it, and will always ask for a better price. Unfortunately, too many service directors/managers and advisors follow the trend, and they automatically think that discounting the repair price (labor and/or parts) is the most effective way to respond to this request. It is undoubtedly the quickest and easiest one, but unfortunately not the most effective one. Negotiating does not always imply "price." Although price is a factor in virtually every sale, it is not usually the primary or motivating factor. Your attitude and the things you say during the first encounter with the customer will determine the value of your service in his/her mind. That is why I believe that it is crucial to consider the negotiation process in order to arrive at better results.

First of all, establish the value of your services. Positioning is an important factor and will affect the price your customer is willing to pay. Compare the services you offer, and the work quality you deliver versus your competitors'. Then, educate your customers. Today's customers are smart; they know what is important and what is not. They know what they want. If you explain to your customers, for example, that your company's goal is to deliver the best work quality in town, and that this is undertaken by hiring certified master technicians only, who receive a "factory-training" on a regular basis, they will understand the reason for which you don't give discounts on labor. They don't want cheap work, either. They know the consequences!

It is hard to foresee the negative effects of discounts to your bottom line, until you compute them. Let's look at this example:

Labor Sales	$500,000	Labor Sales	$500,000
Discount (0%)	$0.00	Discount (10%)	$50,000
Cost of Labor	$125,000	Cost of Labor	$125,000
Gross Profit	**$375,000 (75%)**	**Gross Profit**	**$325,000 (65%)**
Selling Expenses	$50,000	Selling Expenses	$50,000
Employment Exp.	$110,000	Employment Exp.	$110,000
Semi-Fixed Exp.	$50,000	Semi-Fixed Exp.	$50,000
Fixed Expenses	$15,000	Fixed Expenses	$15,000
Occupancy Exp.	$30,000	Occupancy Exp.	$30,000
Operating Profit	**$120,000 (24%)**	**Operating Profit**	**$70,000 (14%)**

As you can see, the G.P. drops from 75% to 65%, but look at the operating profit. It has dropped off 10 points!

If this example does not convince you, just think: What additional Labor Sales would be needed to compensate for the discount?

It can be done by using the simple "break-even" formula: total expenses (including discounts) divided by initial Gross Profit rate. In our example: Labor Sales = $500,000 – Operating Profit = $70,000 = Total expenses or $430,000 / 75% = $573,333! So you need to make at least an extra $73,333 in Labor Sales to compensate for a $50,000 discount! This is an extra 733 hours with an Effective Labor Rate of $100!

Awhile ago, I presented this discount module to an automobile dealer principal: he was amazed by the results. Following the presentation, and to discourage his employees from granting discounts to customers, he decided to provide service managers, service advisors, parts counterpersons, with a reminder showing what percentage of extra sales is needed to compensate for a given discount.

I established the chart in Figure 13-1, and I strongly encourage you to hand in a copy to your front line employees as this dealer principal did.

				YOUR GROSS MARGIN RATE					
	50%	45%	40%	35%	30%	25%	20%	15%	10%
1%	2%	2%	3%	3%	3%	4%	5%	7%	11%
2%	4%	5%	5%	6%	7%	9%	11%	15%	25%
3%	6%	7%	8%	9%	11%	14%	18%	25%	43%
4%	9%	10%	11%	13%	15%	19%	25%	36%	67%
5%	11%	13%	14%	17%	20%	25%	33%	50%	100%
6%	14%	15%	18%	21%	25%	32%	43%	67%	150%
7%	16%	18%	21%	25%	30%	39%	54%	88%	233%
8%	19%	22%	25%	30%	36%	47%	67%	114%	400%
9%	22%	25%	29%	35%	43%	56%	82%	150%	900%
10%	25%	29%	33%	40%	50%	67%	100%	200%	
11%	28%	32%	38%	46%	58%	79%	122%	275%	
12%	32%	36%	43%	52%	67%	92%	150%	400%	
13%	35%	41%	48%	59%	76%	108%	186%	650%	
14%	39%	45%	54%	67%	88%	127%	233%	1400%	
15%	43%	50%	60%	75%	100%	150%	300%		
16%	47%	55%	67%	84%	114%	178%	400%		
17%	52%	61%	74%	94%	131%	213%	567%		
18%	56%	67%	82%	106%	150%	257%	900%		
19%	61%	73%	90%	119%	173%	317%	1900%		
20%	67%	80%	100%	133%	200%	400%	www.FirstAutomobileConsultants.com		

Discount given to customer (%)

TABLE 13-1 Gross Margin rate VS discount rate chart.

How to read this chart? It's easy. In the most left column are the discount rates granted to customers. On the top row are your Gross Margin rates. The numbers on the chart represent the extra sales needed to compensate for the given discount.

Example: If your Gross Margin is 30%, and you consent to a discount of 15%, at the intersection of the 15% row and the 30% column, you find that **100% extra sales are needed to compensate for the discount!**

I hope I convinced you this time. Do not be tempted to give discounts. Teach your employees to stay away from discounts on labor. Every time you discount your services you discount yourself and eat away your profits!

Chapter 14

BREAK-EVEN

Throughout my career, I have noticed that although the break-even formula is widely used by parts managers, only a few service directors/managers use this simple yet powerful formula.

How can you tell if your new idea will have a profitable outcome? The honest answer is, you can't. But this uncertainty shouldn't keep you from researching the financial soundness of your idea. Preparing what's known as a "break-even analysis" can help you determine whether or not your idea is worth it.

Let's briefly review what a break-even point is. The break-even point determines the amount of revenue that should be brought in to cover your expenses before you generate any profit. From a formula standpoint, it would read like this: Fixed Costs / Gross Profit Margin Rate.

Before we go any further, I would like to clarify the

difference between Mark-up and Profit Margin Rate:

- The Mark-up, as its name indicates, marks up a price (cost price) to bring it to a selling price. Let's say that you purchase a part for $5.00. If you mark it up by 1.50, your resulting selling price is $7.50 ($5.00 X 1.50). The Mark-up is **1.50**.
- The Profit Margin on this part is: $7.50 - $5.00 = **$2.50**. The Profit Margin Percentage or Rate is $2.50/ $7.50 = 0.3333 X 100 = **33.33%.**

This being said, let's go back to the break-even point by analyzing a simple example: Your parts department purchases a part for $50.00, sells it for $100.00, and makes a profit of $50.00. The Gross Profit Rate is: $50.00 / $100.00 = 0.500 X 100 = 50.00%.

The parts department Monthly Fixed Costs are $15,000, the break-even point will be $15,000 / 50% = $30,000. This is the amount of revenue needed to cover the expenses.

Now, imagine that the parts manager wants to know how many of these parts would need to be sold to cover the expenses: $15,000 / ($50.00 profit) = 300 parts.

Many experienced entrepreneurs use a break-even analysis as a primary screening tool for new opportunities. These entrepreneurs won't spend time writing a business plan unless the break-even analysis shows that the projected sales revenue exceeds the costs of doing business.

Now, let's see how you can apply this formula in your service department:

- **To evaluate the Labor Sales necessary to cover your expenses**: Consider that you make a Labor Gross Profit Rate of 75%, and that the service department's Average Monthly Fixed Costs are $50,000. What should the Labor Sales be in order to cover your expenses? $50,000 / 75% = **$66,666**.

- **To evaluate the hours necessary to be sold to cover your expenses**: Say that your Effective Labor Rate is $100.00, the Hourly Labor Cost is $45.00; thus, your profit per hour is ($100.00 - $45.00) = $55.00. Your Average Monthly Fixed Costs are $50,000. How many hours are required to be sold to cover your expenses? $50,000 / ($55.00 profit) = **909 hours**.

- **To add an employee**: You plan to hire a second service manager; this change will cost you $80,000 per year. Your actual Average Monthly Fixed Costs are $50,000 and your actual Labor Gross Profit Rate is 75%; you would like to keep your actual Labor Gross Profit Rate in its current state. What monthly Labor Sales are required to cover your actual expenses plus the cost of the newly hired service manager? ($50,000 + $80,000/12) = 56,666 / 75% = **$75,555**.

- **To add any fixed expense**: Your shop is too small to provide its services for the actual volume of cars, and you plan to rent a second facility that will cost you $5,000 per month. Your actual average Monthly Fixed Costs are $50,000, your actual Labor Gross Profit Rate is 70%, and you would like to keep it in its current state. What monthly Labor

Sales are required to cover your actual expenses plus the cost of the new facility? ($50,000 + $5,000) = $55,000 / 70% = **$78,571**.

- **To add Profit to an existing one**: Let's say that you want to make an additional Gross Profit of $10,000: the actual Labor Gross Profit is 65%, and the service department's average Monthly Fixed Costs are $50,000. What Labor Sales will be required to reach your goal? $50,000 (Monthly Costs) + $10,000 (additional profit) = $60,000 / 65% = **$92,307**.

- **To modify your Labor Gross Profit Rate**: Consider that your actual Labor Gross Profit Rate is 65%, and that you would like to bring it to 70%. The service department's average Monthly Fixed Costs are $50,000. What Labor Sales will be necessary to reach your goal? $50,000 / 70% (new GP Rate) = **$71,428**.

I just listed a few instances in which the formula can be used in service departments. It is simple, quick, and pretty accurate. Use it!

You will also appreciate it when preparing your annual objectives, or when you want to know if your inspiring idea will be profitable!

To make your life easier, you can download a specific break-even calculator at www.FirstAutomobileConsultants.com for a minimal charge.

Chapter 15

MATRIX PRICING

Lots of my customers question me about the Matrix Pricing method. This method has been around for a while in the world of wholesale distribution, but is not very popular in automobile dealerships, probably because of its complexity. Some dealerships use the Matrix Pricing method in parts departments, where its use is logical for low-priced items, but I have encountered very few service departments that actually use it. The basic and logical idea behind this pricing method is to increase the selling price in inverse proportion to the cost. More specifically, your margin decreases as the price increases.

I agree that today's speed of life puts an emphasis on time, and rarely do customers waste their time shopping around for an item that is known to be inexpensive; they just buy it when it is needed! I mentioned previously that using this method in parts department is logical. It makes sense for several reasons:

- Parts that are inexpensive represent the majority of sales and the majority of the inventory.

- The cost of the transaction is similar to a far more costly part. The parts counterperson will basically spend the same time to pick up a $0.05 part than a $150.00 part. The booker and cashier will spend the same time in both cases.

The Matrix Pricing method compensates these costs by applying a higher coefficient on a low-cost part and a lower coefficient on a more expensive one. A Matrix Pricing system would break down all parts based on unit cost. For example:

- Cost range from $0.01 to $1.00, cost price X 3.00
- Cost range from $1.01 to $5.00, cost price X 2.75
- Cost range from $5.01 to $10.00, cost price X 2.50
- Cost range from $10.01 to $20.00, cost price X 2.25
- Cost range from $20.01 to $30.00, cost price X 2.00
- Cost over $30.00, Manufacturer Suggested List Price.

Let's compare both methods:

For this example, we are going to use a cost per transaction of $5.00, a part purchased by the dealer for $8.00, and a parts department gross profit of 35%.

- With the "classic" method, the customer pays an amount of $12.30 for the part. The Part Gross Profit is $4.30 ($12.30 - $8.00). **A loss of $0.70 ($4.30 - $5.00) for the dealership!**
- With the Matrix Pricing method, the customer pays

an amount of $20.00 ($8.00 X 2.50) for the part. The Part Gross Profit is $12.00 ($20.00 -$8.00). **And the dealership makes a profit of $7.00 ($12.00 - $5.00) on the transaction!**

It is acceptable for the customer to pay an amount of $20.00 instead of the amount of $12.30. It's not a big deal! Now, do the math with a part that the dealer purchases for $30.00.

With the "classic" method, the customer will pay $46.00 for the part, versus $60.00 with the Matrix Pricing method. As a customer, I would not have liked it!

If you intend to use the Matrix Pricing method in your parts department, calculate your cost per transaction by dividing the Parts Department Total Cost by the number of transactions made for the same period; the result should be close to the one used in our example. But I would recommend limiting the matrix for parts with a cost lower than $15.00.

Regarding service departments, imagine yourself applying the Matrix Pricing method to labor operations. As discussed in Chapter 1, *Everything Is About Hours*, most dealerships and service dealers increase the Manufacturer Suggested Repair Time (MSRT) by a coefficient. We found a range going from 1.2 to 2.5, and even more in some countries.

By using this method, a short operation of 0.50 hour becomes 0.75 hour (0.50 X 1.5), and the customer will pay $75.00 instead of $50.00, but also a longer operation of 15 hours becomes 22.50 hours (15 X 1.5). If the posted Labor

Rate is $100, the cost will jump from $1,500 (MSRT) to $2,250. The customer will be over-billed by 50%!

Here again, even though this method uses a fixed coefficient, we are in the same situation as with the Matrix Pricing method. Both methods are acceptable for short operations, but unacceptable for longer ones. If you are adept at Matrix Pricing, you probably think that when your technician performs a repair where the MSRT gives 0.50 hour, the reality is that the service advisor has already spent 15 minutes with the customer, and that the technician has spent 5 minutes cleaning his hands from a previous job before entering the vehicle in the shop, then spent another 5 minutes to prepare the tools needed to perform the repair; if the technician was efficient, he probably spent an extra 20 minutes to do the job. On top of this, the parts counterperson spent 5 additional minutes to get the parts, and the billing department, 5 additional to prepare the bill; in the best case, 55 minutes (15+5+5+20+5+5) or 0.92 hour (55/60) were spent by your personnel to charge 0.50 hour to the customer, and you are right! That is the reason I believe that if you want to use the Matrix Pricing system for labor operations, it should be used only for short operations.

If you want to elaborate a Matrix Pricing method for labor operations, below are the steps you will need to go through:

- Start with the total Labor Sales for the period (last month to last 3 months, the longer the better).
- Then, evaluate the Total Hours Sold for the same period.
- From there, calculate the actual Effective Labor Rate (Total Labor Sales/Total Hours Sold).

- Evaluate the Cost of Labor
- Then, calculate the Labor Gross Profit Rate.
- Then, record the actual coefficient applied over the MSRT.
- Next, prepare a list of labor time ranges. Start with 0 to 0.50 hour. This is your first range, then increase times by increments of 0.25 hour (0.51 to 0.75; 0.76 to 1.00, etc) up to 15.00 hours, to create additional ranges.
- Next, for the same period, from the repair orders, record the hours sold per labor time range that you have created.
- Then, report the hours sold per range at MSRT value by dividing them by MSRT mark-up coefficient used.
- Evaluate the number of hours superior to 10 hours.
- Since you are going to sell operations superior to 10 hours at MSRT values, deduct them from the Total Hours Sold, and you will have the number of hours below the 10 hours range needed for the matrix to keep the same Labor Gross Profit and compensate the hours superior to the 10 hours range that you are going to sell at MSRT values.
- Then, evaluate the number of hours below 10 sold at MSRT.
- From there, calculate the average mark-up needed for the hours below 10, by dividing the hours needed for the matrix by the number of hours below 10 at MSRT.
- The next step will be to calculate the range increment, by dividing the average mark-up minus 1, by half the number of ranges of operations below 10 hours.

- Then, calculate the highest matrix value (that will be applied to the lowest labor operation range) by adding the increment multiplied by half the number of ranges to the average mark-up.
- Deduct the increment from the highest matrix value to have the matrix for the next operation range, and continue until the last labor operation is inferior or equal to 10 hours.
- Next, apply the matrix to each MSRT range.
- Finally, explain to your technicians that they will be paid based on the MSRT increased by a coefficient that decreases as the labor time increases.

Let's take an example:

- Labor Sales period: $500,000.
- Total Hours Sold: 5,000.
- Effective Labor Rate: $100.
- Cost of Labor: $125,000.
- Labor Gross Profit Rate: 75%
- Mark-up coefficient applied to MSRT: 1.5
- Total Hours Sold superior to 10 at MSRT : (870 : 1.5) = 580
- Total Hours Sold at MSRT : (5,000 : 1.5) = 3,333
- Number of labor operation ranges below 10 hours: 39

Labor operations below 10 hour needed for matrix: (5,000 - 580) = 4,420.
Labor operations < 10 hour sold at MSRT: (3,333 – 580) = 2,753
Average Mark-up for labor operations < 10 hours: 4,420 : 2,753 = 1.605

Range increment: $(1.605 - 1) = 0.605 : (39 : 2) = 19.50 \sim$
$0.605 : 19.50 = 0.0310$
Highest Matrix value: $1.605 + (0.0310 \times 19.50) = 2.2095$
Matrix for first range (labor operations from 0.01 to 0.50 hours MSRT) = 2.21
Matrix for second range (labor operations from 0.51 to 1.00 hour MSRT) = $2.21 - 0.0310 = 2.18$.
Labor operation with Matrix: $0.50 \times 2.21 = 1.10$
Labor operation with Matrix: $0.55 \times 2.18 = 1.19$

Keep applying the matrix to each MSRT range up to 10 hours. It surely looks complicated, but by using this method, you will be close to your actual Labor Sales, Labor Gross Profit, and Total Sold Hours.

If you do not have the time and/or do not want the aggravation of making your own matrix, you can download a ready-to-use Microsoft Excel™ spreadsheet template for this purpose from www.FirstAutomobileConsultants.com. at a minimal cost. The file is called "Matrix_Pricing."

Chapter 16

FINANCIAL STATEMENTS

Your first reaction will probably be to think that as a service director/manager, you do not have to deal with financial statements, and that they are reserved for the dealer principal and the accounting department. If you do not receive a copy on a monthly basis, we urge you to get one. You CANNOT manage your department efficiently without them!

On a monthly basis, ask your dealer principal to provide you with a copy of your department's financial statements. That's right, the only other financial information you need is the share of the total dealership operating profit your department accounts for. Also request a copy of the chart of accounts, since most financial statements use account numbers instead of account names; it will help you understand your expenses. Now, if your dealer principal gives you a copy of all department statements, it is much better to compare how your department performs in comparison to the other departments. But remember that it is not necessary for you to manage your department efficiently. Don't push to get these other financial statements if you feel that the upper management does not wish to release them.

Understanding financial statements is a critical aspect to the success of your department. Analyzing complete financial statements is beyond the scope of this chapter. We will analyze only the part regarding the service department, but first let us quickly review financial statements.

The primary financial statements are represented in the balance sheet, as well as the income statement.

- **The balance sheet** is a snapshot of the company's financial standing at a given time. The balance sheet shows the company's financial position, its assets, liabilities, and net worth. At the "bottom line" of a balance sheet, the values of the assets must always be in balance with the sum of the liabilities values and the net worth values (i.e. assets = liabilities + net worth). The individual elements of a balance sheet change from day to day and reflect the activities of the company. Analyzing how the balance sheet changes over time will reveal important information about the company's business trends.
- **The income statement,** also called the "profit and loss statement," shows all income and expense accounts over a period of time. It shows how profitable the business is. These financial statements show how much money the company will make after all expenses are accounted for. Income statements represent earnings and expenses over a period of time.

Now, let's review the one that interests us the most as service director/manager: the income statement of the **service department**. Depending on the Dealer Management System used at your dealership, the monthly statement printed by your accounting department will look different from the one described in this chapter. Some are more detailed than others are, but you will find basically the same accounts.

You read the statement from top to bottom, and from left to right. The left column indicates the account names or numbers. The next columns show the last three, four, or more months. The current month is usually shown in the second column. In our example, for each month, there is a column that displays the percentage that the account represents. Unfortunately, some statements we have analyzed do not show the column percent; it is a shame because it is the most important reference you have to compare with previous months and/or with the industry average. When a statement doesn't show the column "percent," it means that you have to do it manually, which can be tiresome and time consuming. If your statement doesn't show that column, discuss with your DMS administrator how to get that column.

The statement is divided into categories, and each category contains a list of detailed accounts. Let's start by the categories usually found on the statement:

- **Sales:** the income line that shows labor and usually shop supplies sales as well.
- **Cost of Sales**: the expenses directly related to sales, like labor and shop supplies.
- **Gross Profit**: the result of sales – Cost of Sales.

- **Selling expenses**: the sum of all direct and indirect selling expenses and all general and administrative expenses of your department. Selling expenses are expenses that can be directly linked to sales such as spiffs, credit, warranty, and advertising expenses. Indirect selling expenses are expenses that cannot be directly linked to sales but are proportionally allocated, such as car rentals, etc.
- **Employment expenses**, as indicated by its name, show employment expenses for your department.
- **Semi-fixed expenses**: shows expenses that are not the same every month, like telephone expenses, outside services, training expenses, etc.
- **Fixed expenses**: usually shows expenses that do not change with the volume of business.
- **Occupancy expenses**: they include rent, building maintenance, share of property taxes, etc.
- **Operating Profit**: the result of the gross profit − (employment expenses + semi-fixed expenses + fixed expenses + occupancy expenses) and it is the bottom line of your service department.

Service Department ~ Income Statement

SALES	June		May		April		March		February		Key
Sales	$720,000	100%	$680,000	100%	$710,000	100%	$680,000	100%	$710,000	100%	Ratio
Cost of Sales	$198,500	28%	$200,000	29%	$210,000	30%	$200,000	29%	$200,000	28%	
Gross Profit	**$521,500**	**72%**	**$480,000**	**71%**	**$500,000**	**70%**	**$480,000**	**71%**	**$510,000**	**72%**	**75%**
SELLING EXPENSES											
Service Commission	$500	0.1%	$1,200	0.2%	$1,000	0.1%	$1,100	0.2%	$1,000	0.1%	
Sales promo	$3,600	0.5%	$3,800	0.6%	$3,600	0.5%	$4,200	0.6%	$3,400	0.5%	
MP Spec	$44,000	6.1%	$43,000	6.3%	$46,000	6.5%	$44,000	6.5%	$46,000	6.5%	
RR Exp	$4,200	0.6%	$2,300	0.3%	$1,900	0.3%	$1,800	0.3%	$2,000	0.3%	
Advertising	$6,400	0.9%	$7,400	1.1%	$6,600	0.9%	$8,200	1.2%	$8,100	1.1%	
Rental Veh. Exp.	$9,000	1.3%	$7,000	1.0%	$8,000	1.1%	$7,500	1.1%	$6,000	0.8%	
Other	$500	0.1%	$2,400	0.4%	$2,000	0.3%	$400	0.1%	$500	0.1%	
Selling Expenses	**$68,200**	**9.5%**	**$67,100**	**9.9%**	**$69,100**	**9.7%**	**$67,200**	**9.9%**	**$67,000**	**9.4%**	**10%**
EMPLOYMENT EXP.											
Management	$40,000	5.6%	$38,000	5.6%	$42,000	5.9%	$41,000	6.0%	$44,000	6.2%	
Wages Clerical	$17,000	2.4%	$18,000	2.6%	$16,000	2.5%	$14,500	2.1%	$16,000	2.3%	
Wages Other	$52,000	7.2%	$52,000	7.6%	$53,000	7.5%	$50,000	7.4%	$54,000	7.6%	
Admin Comp.	$2,600	0.4%	$2,600	0.4%	$2,600	0.4%	$2,600	0.4%	$2,600	0.4%	
Dlr Comp.	$5,100	0.7%	$5,200	0.8%	$4,900	0.7%	$6,800	1.0%	$4,500	0.6%	
Owner's Comp.	$2,000	0.3%	$2,000	0.3%	$2,000	0.3%	$2,000	0.3%	$2,000	0.3%	
Porter/Secretary	$2,200	0.3%	$2,800	0.4%	$2,600	0.4%	$2,800	0.4%	$2,400	0.3%	
Empl. Benefits	$3,500	0.5%	$3,500	0.5%	$3,500	0.5%	$3,500	0.5%	$3,500	0.5%	
Absentee	$16,000	2.2%	$16,000	2.4%	$16,000	2.3%	$16,000	2.4%	$16,000	2.3%	
Taxes	$29,000	4.0%	$25,000	3.7%	$23,000	3.2%	$26,000	3.8%	$25,000	3.5%	
Employment Exp.	**$169,400**	**23.5%**	**$165,100**	**24.3%**	**$167,600**	**23.6%**	**$165,200**	**24.3%**	**$170,000**	**23.9%**	**22%**
SEMI FIXED EXPENSES											
Vehicle	$10,000	1.4%	$9,000	1.3%	$10,000	1.4%	$10,000	1.5%	$11,000	1.5%	
Support	$7,000	1.0%	$6,800	1.0%	$5,600	0.8%	$8,000	1.2%	$5,800	0.8%	
Casualty	$3,600	0.5%	$9,700	1.4%	$8,700	1.2%	$3,500	0.5%	$3,900	0.5%	
Uniforms	$2,700	0.4%	$2,600	0.4%	$2,600	0.4%	$2,700	0.4%	$2,600	0.4%	
GMT Fees	$33,000	4.6%	$33,000	4.9%	$34,000	4.8%	$32,000	4.7%	$38,000	5.4%	
Data processing	$5,400	0.8%	$4,900	0.7%	$7,600	1.1%	$6,600	1.0%	$7,400	1.0%	
Outside Services	$12,000	1.7%	$13,000	1.9%	$12,000	1.7%	$8,500	1.3%	$8,000	1.1%	
Security Fees	$2,600	0.4%	$3,500	0.5%	$2,600	0.4%	$3,900	0.6%	$3,400	0.5%	
Telephone	$3,200	0.4%	$3,100	0.5%	$3,200	0.5%	$3,000	0.4%	$3,200	0.5%	
Training	$3,600	0.5%	$3,800	0.6%	$3,400	0.5%	$3,600	0.5%	$3,400	0.5%	
Other	$2,000	0.3%	$2,800	0.4%	$2,700	0.4%	$2,600	0.4%	$2,500	0.4%	
Total Semi Fixed	**$85,100**	**11.8%**	**$92,200**	**13.6%**	**$92,400**	**13.0%**	**$84,400**	**12.4%**	**$89,200**	**12.6%**	**10%**
FIXED EXPENSES											
Insurance	$12,500	1.7%	$12,500	1.8%	$12,500	1.8%	$12,500	1.8%	$12,500	1.8%	
Repair Equip.	$3,500	0.5%	$4,800	0.7%	$3,800	0.5%	$4,600	0.7%	$3,200	0.5%	
Equip. Rent	$6,000	0.8%	$6,000	0.9%	$6,000	0.8%	$6,000	0.9%	$6,000	0.8%	
Total Fixed	**$22,000**	**3.1%**	**$23,300**	**3.4%**	**$22,300**	**3.1%**	**$23,100**	**3.4%**	**$21,700**	**3.1%**	**3%**
OCCUPANCY EXPENSES											
Rent	$20,000	2.8%	$20,000	2.9%	$20,000	2.8%	$20,000	2.9%	$20,000	2.8%	
Repair & Maint.	$2,200	0.3%	$3,100	0.5%	$3,300	0.5%	$3,400	0.5%	$3,200	0.5%	
Tax	$3,500	0.5%	$3,500	0.5%	$3,500	0.5%	$3,500	0.5%	$3,500	0.5%	
Interest	$5,800	0.8%	$5,800	0.9%	$5,800	0.8%	$5,800	0.9%	$5,800	0.8%	
Utilities	$4,300	0.6%	$4,300	0.6%	$4,000	0.6%	$3,500	0.5%	$4,000	0.6%	
Total Occupancy	**$35,800**	**5.0%**	**$36,700**	**5.4%**	**$36,600**	**5.2%**	**$36,200**	**5.3%**	**$36,500**	**5.1%**	**5%**
Total Expenses	**$380,500**	**52.8%**	**$384,400**	**56.5%**	**$388,000**	**54.6%**	**$376,100**	**55.3%**	**$384,400**	**54.1%**	**50%**
Operating Profit	**$141,000**	**19.6%**	**$95,600**	**14.1%**	**$112,000**	**15.8%**	**$103,900**	**15.3%**	**$125,600**	**17.7%**	**20%**

FIGURE 16-1 Income statement analysis worksheet.

When analyzing the statement, you start with "Sales" and

you compare its value versus the objective; you also compare it to that of previous months. In our example, we have $720,000 for the month of June, and the value is above that of the month of May and that of the month of April. It doesn't mean too much, as long as the objective is met. Let us continue. The column "Percent" starts with 100%, and the percentage of all other accounts will be based on the Sales (i.e. in our example, we have 28% and 72% respectively for Cost of Sales and Gross Profit. This means that the cost of sales is 28% of the Sales, and the GP 72% of the Sales). Then, here again, you compare the "Cost of Sales" value versus its objective and percentage as well as the ones from previous months. In our example, it shows $198,500 in June, and it is below the two previous months. The percentage of 28% is also below that of the three previous months, and it looks good. Don't forget, this is the cost of your labor and shop supplies, and as with all costs, you want to keep them as low as possible, and bring it around 25%.

The most important is of course the "Gross Profit," and in our case, it is the amount of $521,500 and represents 72% of the Sales. When comparing it with previous months, it looks pretty good. Yet, we have found well-managed service departments at 75% and above.

How can you get there?

- Start with repair orders analysis
- Look at your shop's productivity and efficiency
- Make sure you don't lose money on shop supplies
- Check your employee overtime
- Make sure you make adequate profit on external works

You will now analyze the "Selling Expenses," which regroups spiffs, commissions, promotions, advertising, car rental, and other expenses linked to Sales. In our example, we have $68,200 or 9.5% of Sales. Your statement will probably look different because expenses are not necessarily allocated the same way at your dealership. Compare these expenses versus the annual objectives, and pay special attention to the account "Other." This is the account in which your accounting department enters expenses that it cannot enter in a given account. When the amount is low, don't bother, but if the amount is high, ask for details.

Then, check your "Employment Expenses." Here again, depending on your state, internal organization, and DMS used, your statement will look different. In our example, we have $169,400 or 23.5% of Sales. Often, accounts beyond your control will be added mainly for tax purposes, like Owner Compensation, etc. Compare these expenses with the objectives, and pay particular attention to the account titled "Absentee" if it is on your statement. It is the expenses made while your employees are on vacation, or because you are paying these employees who are not physically at your dealership.

Next, the "Semi-Fixed Expenses," the "Fixed Expenses," and the "Occupancy Expenses" are often grouped together within one title. Let's start with the Semi-Fixed Expenses of our example. We have total Fixed Expenses of $85,100 or 11.8% of Sales. Compare each account with the annual objectives, and the average of your manufacturer. Look for discrepancies. Also, pay attention to the account titled "Other"; it should be as all other accounts under the same title, close to nothing. Proceed the same way with Fixed and Occupancy expenses.

Regardless of the DMS and accounting system used at your dealership, you will have the Total expenses line. To obtain a decent Operating Profit, your total expenses should be below 50% of Sales. In our example, we have $380,500 or 52.8% of Sales and an operating profit of $141,000 or 19.6% of Sales.

In conclusion, since your position also requires time for customer satisfaction, quality of work, employee satisfaction, and other duties, you cannot spend too much time analyzing income statements and other financial documents. You want to be able to pinpoint the status of your department in the blink of an eye, and spend time analyzing in detail the statement only when your indicators "tell" you that there is a problem. That is what I call managing by "Key Ratios."

In order to manage your department efficiently, you need to compare these ratios with your annual objectives as well as the industry and/or brand average. For the financial statement, these key ratios are:

- Sales - should match or be above your annual objectives
- Gross profit - should be at least 75% (38% for parts department)
- Operating profit - should be about 20%.
- Service department operating profit - should represent about 1/3 of the total dealership operating profit.
- Since all other expenses will differ depending on your internal organization, the accounting, and the

DMS used at your dealership, we do not give you a ratio for each account. Keep in mind that as long as your sales match or are above the objective, your Labor GP is at least equal to 75%, and your Operating Profit 20%, you are in good shape!

Do not think I encourage you to look at these ratios only. If you are lucky enough and have time to analyze each account, do it! You will definitely improve your bottom line! Also, remember to compare your expenses with the industry average every time it is possible.

Chapter 17

FOLLOW THE TREND

17.1 THE BUSINESS CYCLE

An economy course is beyond the scope of this chapter, but as service director/manager, you know that the economy plays an important role in the development of your business. Yet, how does one take advantage of it? For example, before expanding your service department's capacity, you may wish to know whether a recession is about to hit. This chapter will bring you the knowledge you need to take advantage of the economic situation.

You have already heard the trading sayings "Follow the trend!" or "The trend is your friend!" Unfortunately, the economical situation is beyond your control, but it is not a reason to ignore it. By following the basic economical trends, you will create realistic annual objectives, and make changes in your business or career at the right time!

But let us begin with the business cycle. You have probably

heard the words "Boom; Expansion; Prosperity; Recovery; Contraction; Depression, and Recession" before. They each describe phases and periods of an economy and altogether create a cycle. This cycle is called the Business Cycle.

The Business Cycle is displayed as a sinusoidal line with:

- a **Peak** (the highest point of the line)
- a **Mean** (a middle line between the Peak and the Trough)
- a **Trough** (the lowest point of the line)

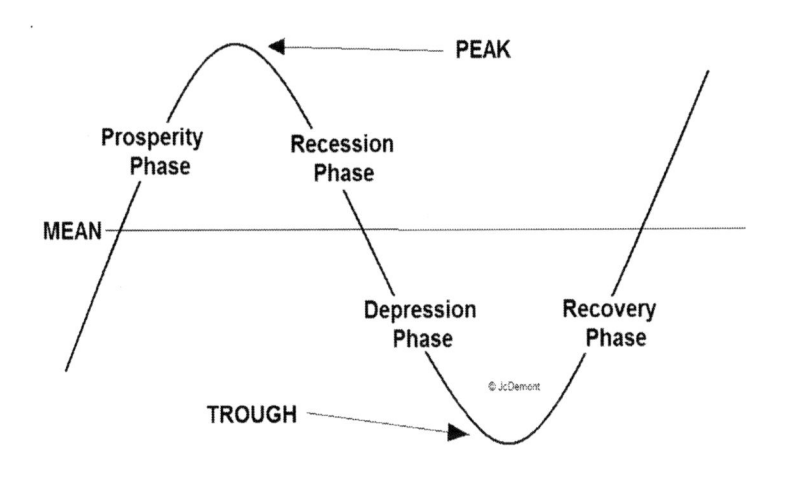

The business cycle includes four phases:

- The **Prosperity** phase, also called the Boom, starts from the **Mean** and lasts until the **Peak** is reached.
- The **Recession** phase follows the **Prosperity** phase, and starts from the **Peak** back to the **Mean**.
- The **Depression** phase is the slide from the **Mean** to the **Trough**.

- The **Recovery** phase is the rise from the **Trough** back to the **Mean**.

These four phases represent two distinct periods:

- The **Expansion period,** which regroups the Recovery and the Prosperity phases (economy is driven upward).
- The **Contraction period,** which comprises the Recession and the Depression phases (economy is driven downward).

The duration of the cycle is evaluated from Peak to Peak or from Trough to Trough, but the result is identical for each. I analyzed over 130 years of business cycles in the US, from 1854 to 1991, and obtained an average of 55 months from Peak to Peak, and also an average of 55 months from Trough to Trough. During the period analyzed, the average business cycle duration was 4 ½ years!

Within the last 20 years (1982-2001), the knowledge of today's economists associated with the evolution of computer technology increased the business cycle to 9 ½ years! Also, during the same period, the length of the expansion period passed from 58 months in 1982 to 120 months in 2001.

You probably think that all this is wonderful, but how can you take advantage of this as a service director/manager in order to benefit from it?

Take a look at some recent US presidents' years, and you will understand how a well-informed individual can take advantage of the business cycle:

- Ronald Reagan took power in 1981, with a few months left to the end of the prosperity phase, then got 18 bad months, and enjoyed 7 years of Recovery and Prosperity (see Figure 17-2). Will he be remembered as a president who did something advantageous for the economy? Sure!
- It is the same situation with Bill Clinton, who took power during the Recovery phase, then spent the rest of his two terms in the Recovery and Prosperity phases (see Figure 17-2). Will he be remembered as a president who did something advantageous for the economy? You bet!

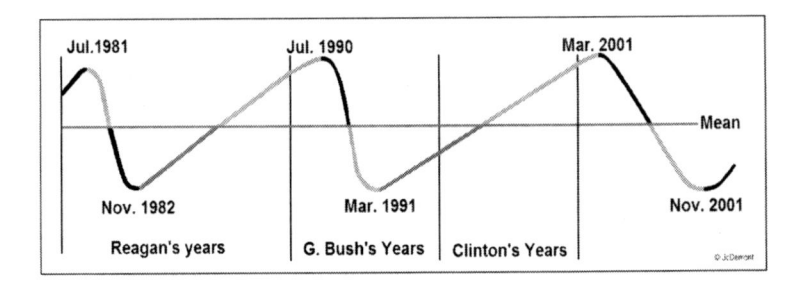

FIGURE 17-2 Relationship between the business cycle, and the U.S. presidents.

- Now, take a look at when President George Bush took power a few months before the end of the Prosperity phase. He then spent his term between Recession and Depression phases, and lost the election just after the Recovery phase started (see Figure 17-2). He probably won't be remembered as the best president for the economy. Is it his fault? No. Timing is everything!

If you can predict when an Expansion period starts, or when a Contraction period starts, don't you think you will have an advantage on your competitors? What happens during the Contraction period? Sales decline, manufacturers reduce the production, employment declines, and incomes decline! If you take a new position at the wrong time, obviously you will have less chance to succeed than if you took it at the right time. Thus, you do not want to make a position change without being fully aware of the business cycle phase in which you are. You should prepare your annual objectives accordingly.

If you are interested in this fascinating subject, I recommend that you read *Beating the Business Cycle*, by Lakshman Achutan and Anirvan Banerji, and if you wish to stay updated, you can subscribe to ECRI (Economic Cycle Research Institute) for less than $20.00 per month (value as of August 2007).

17.2 THE FEDERAL FUNDS RATE

Another important factor of the economy that affects your businesses is the Federal Funds Rate. It is the interest rate at which banks lend money to each other, usually on an overnight basis, and it is used by the government to keep the inflation under control by adding or subtracting reserves of money in order to stabilize the Federal Funds target rate.

Figure 17-3 shows the Federal Funds Rate versus the Inflation Rate from January 1990 to June 2006. It is interesting to see how the Fed controls inflation by increasing or decreasing the Federal Funds Rate.

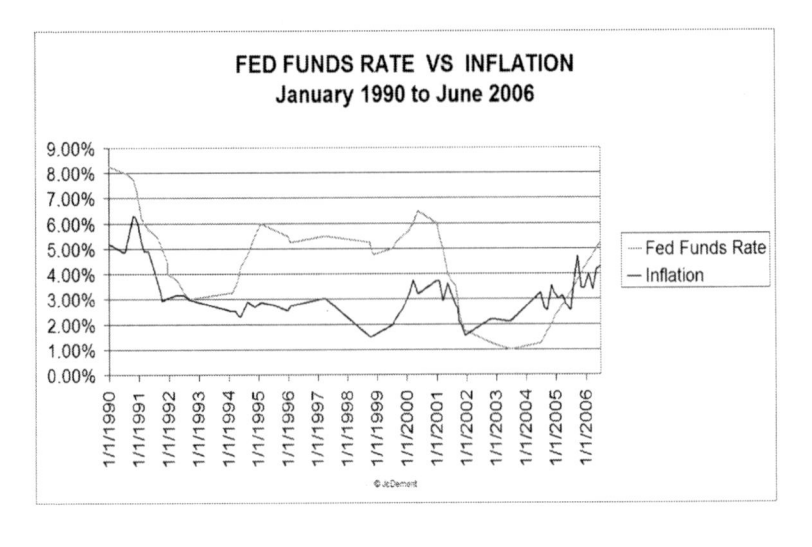

FIGURE 17-3 FED Fund rate VS Inflation Rate chart

When the rate is low, it makes it easier for consumers to purchase vehicles and goods. Do you recall how vehicle manufacturers recently offered consumers 0% interest on new-vehicle purchases? The result: Over 16 millions new cars were sold in the US in 2005. According to the *National Automobile Dealers Association*, the nation's franchised new car and light truck dealers recorded their third strongest year on record in 2005. Will this have a negative impact on your department? Not really, because pre-delivery inspections will be required for new cars, and you will recondition most trade-ins anyway. What will change is the work mix: Internal Work (pre-delivery inspections, pre-owned vehicle repairs) and Warranty Work will increase as Customer Paid Work decreases.

When the rate is high, the effects are mainly reversed.

You can find values and information on the Federal Funds

Rate at www.bankrate.com, and/or at www.federalreserve.gov/fomc/fundsrate.htm

17.3 TAYLOR'S RULE

It is important for every businessman to know in advance when a change in the Federal Funds Rate will probably occur in order to react consequently prior to competitors. This will also enable the business or department manager to take advantage of the upcoming situation. The economist John Taylor wrote a formula known as Taylor's Rule, which does just that.

The rule recommends a high interest rate when inflation is above its target or when the Real GDP is above the Potential GDP, and a relatively low interest rate in the opposite situations. Although the Fed does not explicitly follow Taylor's Rule, it is widely advocated by monetary analysts and policymakers.

Let's take a look at the basic Taylor's Rule: when Real GDP is equal to Potential GDP and inflation is at its target rate of 2 percent, the Fed Funds Rate should be about 4 percent, implying a Real Interest Rate (Equilibrium Rate) of about 2 percent.

If Real GDP rises 1 percent above Potential GDP, the Fed Funds Rate should be raised 0.5 percent relative to the current inflation rate. If inflation rises by 1 percent above the 2 percent target, the Fed Funds Rate should be raised by 0.5 percent relative to the inflation rate.

Here is the formula: Current Inflation Rate + Equilibrium

Rate + 0.5*(Current Inflation Rate – Target Inflation Rate) + 0.5*(Real GDP - Potential GDP)

Let's take a look at a few examples:
Example #1

- Equilibrium Real Interest Rate = 2%
- Actual Inflation Rate = 2%
- Target Inflation Rate = 2%
- Real GDP Growth = 3%
- Potential GDP Growth = 3%
- **Fed fund rate = 4%** (2 + 2) + 0.5*(2-2=0) + 0.5*(3-3=0)

Example #2

- Equilibrium Real Interest Rate = 2%
- Actual Inflation Rate = 4%
- Target Inflation Rate = 2%
- Real GDP Growth = 1%
- Potential GDP Growth = 1%
- **Fed fund rate = 7.0%** (4 + 2) + 0.5*(4-2=2) + 0.5*(1-1=0)

Example #3

- Equilibrium Real Interest Rate = 2%
- Actual Inflation Rate = 1.5%
- Target Inflation Rate = 2%
- Real GDP Growth = 3%
- Potential GDP Growth = 4.77%
- **Fed fund rate = 2.37%** (1.5 + 2) + 0.5*(1.5-2= -0.25) + 0.5*(3-4.77 = -1.77)= -0.885

You can find values and information on the Inflation Rate at www.inflationrate.com.

To simplify your life, you can download for a minimal fee a Fed's Funds Rate Calculator from www.FirstAutomobileConsultants.com.

17.4 THE YIELD CURVE

Another quick way to gauge the economy is by comparing the Long-Term Interest Rate (10-Year Treasury Note) to the Short-Term Interest Rate (3-Month Treasury Bill). Normally, you expect to get more interest paid to you for holding a longer maturity, but in theory there is more risk to holding a bond for 10 years than for 3 months! We analyzed over 40 years of yield spread between the 10-year treasury note and the 3-month treasury bill. Figure 17-4 represents the 3-month average of both, the 10-Year Treasury Note, and the 3-Month Treasury Bill. Each time the yield spread turned negative (short-term rates actually rise above long-term rates) or flirted with zero, a recession followed!

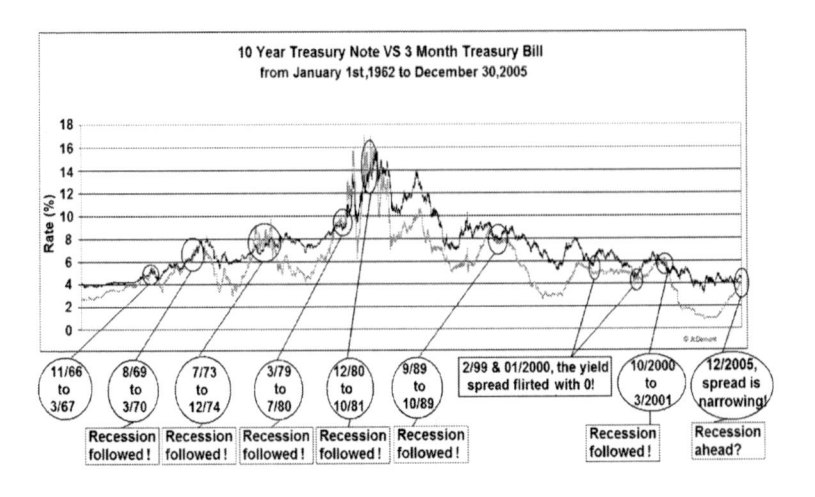

FIGURE 17-4 Long Term Interest Rate VS Short Term
Interest Rate chart.

As you can see on Figure 17-4, at the end of December
2005, the yield spread (gap) between Long-Term and
Short-Term interest is very narrow. Is it an indication of an
upcoming recession? It is not an easy answer! You must
not use only one indicator to predict an economic change.
Now, if several indicators point to the same direction, keep
in mind that there is no smoke without fire!

You can get these rates daily, at
http://www.bloomberg.com/markets/rates/index.html .

17.5 UNEMPLOYMENT RATE

Another important number you want to monitor, because it
will improve your bottom line, is the Unemployment Rate.
As you know, market value is based on supply and demand,
and when the unemployment rate is high, a lot of

employees are on the job market, and it indicates that:

- You have a wider choice of personnel to hire.
- Since there is more personnel on the market than there are job offers, their costs are lower.

Of course, when the unemployment rate is low, it is difficult to find new employees, and their costs will be higher.

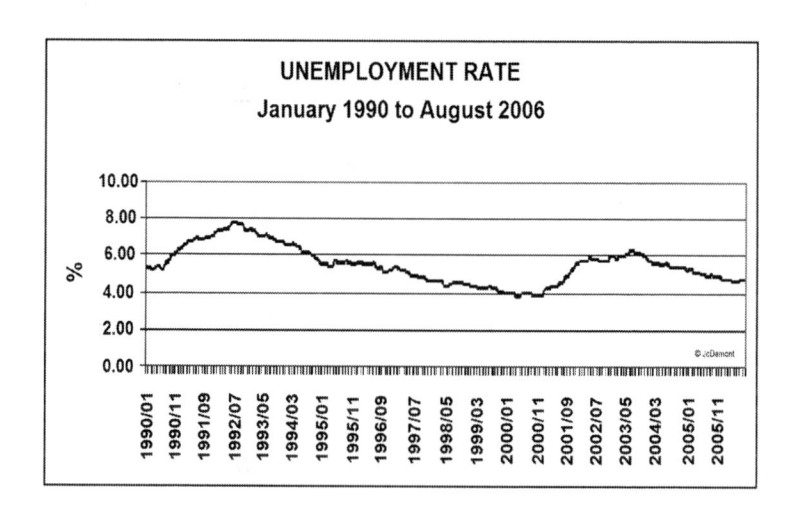

FIGURE 17-5 Unemployment Rate from January 1990 to August 2006.

You must monitor the long-term trend, as shown on Figure 17-5, to take advantage of it and make the right decision to hire new employees, let go of the ones you are not satisfied with, or prevent your good employees from leaving.

You can also evaluate which month is most favorable or most unfavorable to hire employees, by monitoring the monthly average as we did on Figure 17-6. As you can see on that figure: January, February, and July are the best months to hire.

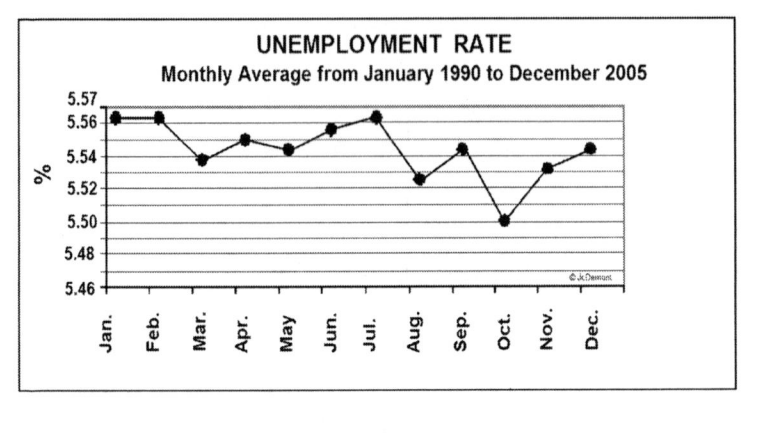

FIGURE 17-6 Monthly unemployment Rate.

By understanding and following the Business Cycle and the Federal Funds Rate, by using the Taylor's Rule, by comparing the yield spread of the long-term interest rate versus the short-term one, and by monitoring the unemployment rate, you should be able to make sound decisions about your business in accordance with the economy.

Remember, as a rule of thumb, never go against the trend!

Chapter 18

SELLING YOURSELF

If you apply everything you have learned in these chapters, there is no doubt you will obtain amazing results! But wait, your job is not done yet! Your next objective will be to "sell yourself" to the upper management and to be rewarded for what you have accomplished. There are quite a number of people who are more qualified than I am, and who have written books concerning the matter; thus, I will only give you a brief overview of the matter without spending too much time discussing it.

If you are doing a good job, and the dealer's principal and its other key representatives are unaware of it, you will not get any credit for your work! My suggestion is that you prepare at least one annual report that you will hand in to the dealer's principal and to the other representatives in upper management as well. This annual report will discuss what you have accomplished during the past year in order to improve customer satisfaction, employee satisfaction, dealer's profits, work quality, etc. Write a short and concise report if you want it to be read! Get to the point: these people generally do not have the time to read a 10-page report from each department manager.

Your report should include at least 4 points:

- Customer satisfaction in the past and present.
- Employee satisfaction in the past and present.
- Dealer's profits in the past and present.
- Work quality in the past and present.

You should also include a quick explanation for each point on what you have done to arrive at the present results. Also, to reinforce your report, you should include a graph to display the progress made.

On a monthly basis, to monitor the progress on each of the above-mentioned points, I used a Microsoft Excel spreadsheet with radar graphs plotted with each one of these points. By focusing your eye on the center point (zero), you can interpret the performance of your workshop for each point (the more area filled, the better it is!). You can include these graphs in your report. Figure 18-1 displays a graph sample.

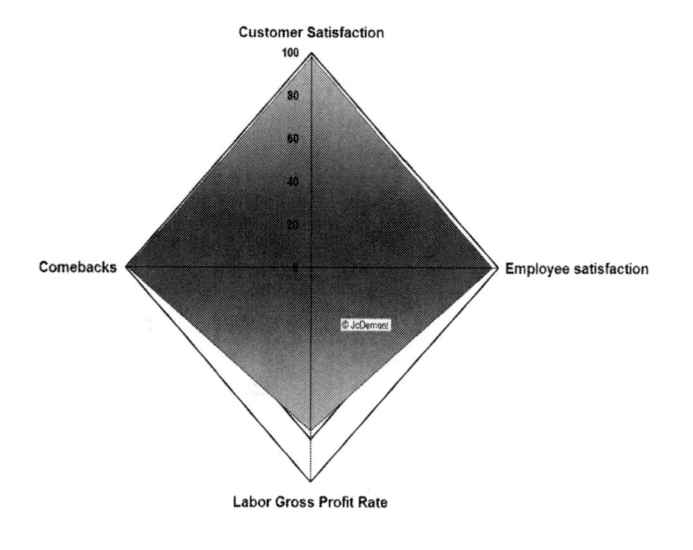

FIGURE 18-1 Service department satisfaction graph.

If you use 4 points to monitor the overall satisfaction of your service department, you can download the MS Excel spreadsheet template for a minimal fee at www.FirstAutomobileConsultants.com. Look for the file named "4PointsRadar."

Glossary

Attendance Hour: The time your technicians are present on the work site. It is obtained by deducting the Fixed Non-Productive Hours from the Available Hours.

Attendance Time: see Attendance Hour.

Available Hour: The time the shop is opened for business multiplied by the number of technicians.

Available Time: see Available Hour.

Break-Even Point: The point at which sales equal expenses. There is no profit made or loss incurred at the Break-Even Point.

Car Park: The total number of cars for the brand(s) you represent sold in your market area for a given time, usually 5 or 10 years.

Comeback: Vehicle returning to the shop for correction or unfinished previous work.

Competitive Analysis: A procedure that evaluates your competitor's strengths and weaknesses.

Competitive Work: Usually includes such items as lube, oil, and filter, alignment, balance, and tire rotation.

Course Credit: A "credit" given in hours, which you earn on the basis of the satisfactory completion of courses.

CRM: See Customer Relationship Management.

CSI: See Customer Satisfaction Index.

Customer Loyalty: Customer's fidelity to your business.

Customer Relationship Management: Software used to store customers' data to address the needs of marketing, sales, and customer service. The purpose of CRM software is to manage the customer through the entire life cycle. Each interaction with a customer is added to a customer's contact history, and staff can retrieve customers' information from the database as necessary. Customers can interact with different people in a company over time without having to repeat the history.

Customer Satisfaction Index: An indicator tracking the quality of products and services from the customer's perspective.

Effective Labor Rate: The total Labor Sales divided by the total Sold Hours. It should be within 10% of your posted labor rate.

Efficiency: The Sold Hours divided by Productive Hours,

given as a percentage. It is an indicator you must monitor because it is the end result of the way your shop is managed. It is obtained by dividing the Sold Hours (total hours billed) by the Productive Hours (the time your technicians work productively).

ELR: see Effective Labor Rate.

Employee Performance Evaluation: A process to evaluate employees' work performance and personal behavior.

Employee Satisfaction Index: An index based on a process to monitor overall employee satisfaction.

Facility Potential: The potential volume of work your facility can absorb, given in hours.

Facility Utilization: The extent to which you use your facility, given as a percentage. It is obtained by dividing the Labor potential (Hours) by the Facility Potential, then multiply the result by 100.

Fixed Non-Productive Hours: Time paid to technicians when they are not present in the shop, such as vacation days, training days, and other planned off-time.

Flat Rate Compensation: A technician paid based on a flat rate billing system.

Flat Rate Hours: A time established by auto manufacturers for a given repair operation used for billing as well as paying purposes for the operations performed.

Flat Rate Manual: A guide established by auto manufacturers for most conceivable repairs. This includes everything from a bulb replacement to installing a new engine.

FRH: see Flat Rate Hours.

GP: Gross Profit. Sales minus Cost of Sales. See also Labor Gross Profit.

Individual Competitive Analysis: See Competitive Analysis.

Job Description: A list of major areas of an employee's job or position.

Labor Gross Profit, or Labor GP: Obtained by subtracting the Cost of Labor from the Labor Sales.

Labor Gross Profit Rate: One of the most important numbers for the service director. It is obtained by dividing the Labor Gross Profit by the Labor Sales, then multiply it by 100.

Labor Potential: The potential volume of labor needed to maintain your car park, given in hours.

Maintenance Work: Labor operations generally recommended by the manufacturer, such as brake, tune-up, scheduled maintenance, filters, and drive belts.

Manufacturer Suggested Repair Time: Time given by the manufacturer to conduct a given repair. Also, used as a base to reimburse warranty work.

Mark-up: Coefficient applied to the cost of a product to obtain its selling price.

Matrix Pricing: A pricing method to increase the selling prices in inverse proportion to the cost. More specifically, your margin decreases as the price increases.

MRT: Manufacturer Repair Time. See Manufacturer Suggested Repair Time.

MSRT: See Manufacturer Suggested Repair Time.

NADA: National Automobile Dealers Association.

Owners Base: See Car Park.

One-Item RO: Repair Order with only one line charged to the customer.

Pay Plan: A management tool that enables the manager to control personnel cost, which increases employees' morale and reduces work force turnover by rewarding employees for their contributions to the success of the service department.

Posted Labor Rate: The hourly labor rate charged to customers.

Productive Hours: The time the technicians are available to work. It is obtained by deducting Variable Non-Productive Hours from the Attendance Hours.

Productivity: The Productive Hours divided by the Available Hours, given as a percentage. It is the first indicator you must monitor because it gives you an idea of the loss caused by the non-productive time (fixed and variable). It is obtained by dividing the Productive Hours (the time your technicians work productively) by the Available Hours (the time the shop is open for business).

Proficiency: The Sold Hours divided by the Available Hours, given as a percentage. It combines productivity and efficiency, and it is a quick and powerful indicator to gauge the health of the entire shop or a technician's output.

Repair Order: A document filled out by the service advisor, and *signed_*by the customer. It is the only link between the customer's request and the technician. It is also a contract between the customer and the service department!

Repair Time: See Manufacturer Suggested Repair Time.

RO: See Repair Order.

Sales Potential: The potential sales amount based on your car park.

Scrap Rate: Each year, several vehicles are destroyed and scrapped. The rate is obtained by dividing the total of those vehicles by the total of vehicles sold during the same period, and then multiplied by 100.

Segment 1: Cars up to 4 year old.

Segment 2: Cars between 5 and 7 years old.

Segment 3: Cars between 8 and 10 years old.

Service Cycle Analysis: The evaluation of each step your customers have to go through, such as Appointment; Reception; Repair; Quality Control; Invoicing; Vehicle Handover; and Follow-up.

Service Market Analysis: Evaluate the labor and parts sales potential to maintain a given car park.

Service Market Potential: See service market analysis.

Shop Supplies: Small cost items (bolts, nuts, pins, etc.) used in the shop on a daily basis.

Sold Hours: The hours billed by your department to customers, manufacturers, and to your company's other departments.

Spiff: A word that has been in use in the sales and marketing business, and defines a small bonus for an additional sale.

SRT: Suggested Repair Time. See Manufacturer Suggested Repair Time.

Technician Utilization: The Technician Productive Hours divided by Attendance Hours. It is an important indicator in shop management because it gives you a pretty good idea of the way your technicians are busy. It is given as a percentage.

Training Needs Evaluation: A procedure to evaluate the staff's training needs.

Variable Labor Rates: When two or more labor rates are

offered to the customer, according to the level of difficulty of the work performed.

Variable Non-Productive Hours: The time wasted by technicians between jobs, either waiting for parts, or other non-productive tasks.

Printed in the United Kingdom
by Lightning Source UK Ltd.
134462UK00001B/229/P

9 781432 718701